LEGENDS & LORE
ALONG CALIFORNIA'S
HIGHWAY 395

LEGENDS & LORE
ALONG CALIFORNIA'S
HIGHWAY 395

BRIAN CLUNE
With Photography by Terri Clune

THE
History
PRESS

Published by The History Press
Charleston, SC
www.historypress.com

Front cover, top left: Courtesy of Colonel Vernon P. Saxon Jr. Aerospace Museum; *top right*: Courtesy of Mono Basin Historical Society.
Back cover, top: Courtesy of Mono Basin Historical Society.

Unless otherwise noted, all photos are courtesy of Terri Clune.

First published 2022

Manufactured in the United States

ISBN 9781467151061

Library of Congress Control Number: 2021949174

Notice: The information in this book is true and complete to the best of our knowledge. It is offered without guarantee on the part of the author or The History Press. The author and The History Press disclaim all liability in connection with the use of this book.

A trip down Highway 395 takes you from desert scrub…

…to lush Sierra Alpine forest vistas.

Writing this book was as challenging, if not more so, than it was for *Haunted Heart of San Diego*. The reason is the COVID-19 pandemic and the difficulties in talking with people and being able to access locations. With this in mind, I want to again thank all of the selfless individuals who daily put themselves in harm's way, both physically and medically, to keep the rest of us safe. Also, with the world again becoming a more dangerous place, I want to thank all of the men and women in the armed forces of the United States for their dedication and the sacrifices they endure to keep America, and the world, safe and free.

From pine-scented forests, past boulders and streams, to clear lakes encircled by murals and dreams.
Where bright clouds emblazon a warm azure sky, a trail through mountains is one I must try.

—excerpt from the poem "The Mountains Are Calling"
by Edward A. Morris as a tribute to John Muir

CONTENTS

Contents

ACKNOWLEDGEMENTS

There are so many people I have met and spoken with on the journey of writing this book that it would take more pages than I can spare to mention them all. I want to thank all of those who took the time to give me the stories, histories and legends of this amazing roadway. You will never know how much it means to me. The people of the Owens Valley and Eastern Sierra are truly wonderful, and I highly recommend getting to know them when you are road-tripping the El Camino Sierra. Special thanks go out to author Danielle Nadler, who took the time out of her busy life so I could interview her and sent me her wonderful book *Without a Trace* so I could get to know a man who is truly a legend of the area, the Sierra Phantom. I need to thank my nephew Curren Clune, who hiked with me in the Sierra to get photos for the book. Some of the hikes were, shall we say, grueling. Thanks also go out to Rob and Candy Weil of Sierra Strange in Bridgeport, California, for allowing me to monopolize their time (and their shop) while asking for more and more stories of high strangeness. Again, thanks to Laurie Krill, my acquisitions editor, along with all of those at Arcadia/The History Press who make me look much better than I am. Of course, I would be remiss if I left out my wife, Terri, who accompanies me on these adventures, edits my sloppy words, took all of the photos and is the best friend a man could ask for.

INTRODUCTION

Tell people from California that you will be driving the Pacific Coast Highway, the 5 freeway or the 15, and they will say, "Oh I love the coast route," or, "Oh, going up to San Francisco?" or, "Heading to Vegas?" Tell them you are driving Highway 395, and most will look at you with a blank stare and ask, "Where does that go?" There are those who know this road well, such as skiers, fishermen and gamblers heading to Reno or avid ghost towners. But those unfamiliar with this stretch of highway are truly missing out on one of the great road trips California has to offer.

US 395 used to run from San Diego to the Nevada border, but when Interstate 15 was completed, the southern section was absorbed by the new freeway. Now, 395 runs from the City of Victorville, north through Kern County and the Owens Valley, then on into Carson City, Nevada, and north from there. The parts of this roadway in California have some of the most spectacular views one could hope for on a road trip. Majestic mountains, lonely deserts, historic monuments and ghost towns dot the highway in an unending cascade of beauty and lost dreams. US 395 also has its fair share of kitsch.

From toilet seats to size 14 shoes, tunnels to nowhere and strange cryptids, even a ghost or two, Highway 395 has it all. From the small town of Lone Pine, one can travel to the highest point in the contiguous United States just a few minutes out of town or to the lowest point only an hour or so away in Death Valley. You can travel to the now dry Owens Lake, the victim of a thirsty Los Angeles population, past alpine waters teeming with life, or to the dead, sulfur-infused waters and tufas of Mono Lake. The highway becomes a fisherman's dream during the spring and summer, while in the winter, Mammoth Mountain becomes a playground for skiers, snowboarders and those who love to sip toddies in the hot tub.

The road has small towns and small cities, ghost towns and semi–ghost towns. There are historical monuments and vestiges from a time we wish we could forget but know we cannot, for fear they may happen again. Relics hearken back to a simpler time we wish we could revisit.

All of this awaits you on the road sometimes called "Death Alley" for its many long, straight drives that lull one to sleep. There is even more to see for those who look around and view the wonders this stretch of highway has to offer. So, sit back and enjoy all of the legends and lore this amazing drive—also known as the El Camino Sierra—has in store for you!

PART I

FASCINATING CHARACTERS ALONG THE HIGHWAY

1

GEORGE "WALKING MAN" SWAIN

T he tiny mining town of Boron, just off of the 395 in Kern County, is a town easily missed. The town is home to the largest borax mine in the world. Borax has so many uses that it would be hard to mention them all, but most people will recognize it from the many cleaning products that include borax. Other people, especially older generations, may also remember the Twenty Mule Team Borax company and logo. With a population of just over two thousand people, and located in the middle of a desert landscape, Boron is not the type of place one sets out for. Rather, one ends up there. This may not be such a bad thing, however.

Boron has plenty to offer the traveler for a whole day exploring its historic and sometimes odd sights. There is the Twenty Mule Team Museum, with its animatronic twenty-mule team pulling a wagon train of borax. The wheels turn, the driver pumps his arms to get the team moving and the mules bounce; their heads bob and their ears flop. It's truly a sight worthy of any roadside attraction.

Along with the Twenty Mule Team Museum, Boron is also home to the Saxon Aerospace Museum, which honors nearby Edwards Air Force Base. One can also tour the Rio Tinto Borax Mine Visitor Center, where visitors can learn all about borax mining. There are concrete tortoises, a barrel-shaped food stand and the Boron History Museum. At this museum you can learn about two locals who, in their own right, have become legends not only in Boron but also beyond.

This animatronic Twenty Mule Team still operates as well today as it did more than sixty years ago.

George Wood Swain became a legend within Kern County, but not for any great deed or derring-do. Swain became a legend because he liked to walk! He was an avid opera fan with a photographic memory and a degree from Stanford University. He had three passions in life. The first was classical music. His mother had taught him to play the piano and organ at an early age. The second passion was John Muir. And the third was conservation of the environment, most likely a result of the lessons he learned from Muir. Maybe it was his love of the land that led Swain to forgo most forms of transportation other than his unusually large feet. But whatever it may have been, Swain preferred to get around in his size 14EEE boots.

George began working as a chemist at the Pacific Borax Company on April 4, 1944 (4/4/44), and he retired on August 8, 1988 (8/8/88). This was not an accident but a planned joke by Swain. Living on the edge of the Mojave Desert takes a stout individual. Extreme high temperatures during the day can turn into very cold temperatures at night, and the lack of any measurable rain can make one think they have landed in the pit of hell. This is if you live in a comfortable home with modern amenities. Think what it must have been like if you lived in abandoned borax workers' cabins. If it became extremely cold in the desert environment, Swain would stay in the

Boron Motel. In 1993, Swain lived almost exclusively in the motel or, on other occasions, would house-sit for friends while they were away.

Not only did George never own a car but he also never owned a house. Swain would find an old, abandoned miner's shack that wasn't in deplorable condition and move in. He would live there until it became uninhabitable or fell prey to the elements and then find another place to lay his head. Swain wore clothing that made him look like a tramp, but he was anything but. Swain was often seen walking around Boron, carrying a box and picking up trash and recyclables. The kids around town would often help him pick things up, and they began calling him "Walking George." Over time, the name stuck, and he became known as "Walking George" Swain.

Regardless of how Swain dressed, he was not without means. Never having been married, with no rent, no car and no house or property maintenance to pay for, George saved most of his paycheck. He didn't let his money collect dust, however. The "Walking Man" was generous, helping anyone he ran across who needed it. Those who were homeless, helpless or hopeless always found Walking George there to help. One year, he even personally funded the Seattle Opera Company for a season when it was so strapped for cash that it almost had to close.

George Swain liked to walk. He would walk to and from work daily, walk to the store or anywhere else in town he needed to go. He also walked much farther. Walking George loved to trek out to Death Valley, a more than one-hundred-mile walk, round trip. He would often step out to the old Boron Federal Prison five miles away from his home just to chat with the prison administrator and would walk thirty miles into the town of Mojave to catch a bus to the city or up to the Yosemite area to attend the annual John Muir Memorial Association dinner. In the twenty-five years Swain was an active member, he never missed this annual event.

George also loved train travel. He often took trips around the country just to enjoy a train ride and see America. He was often heard around town reminiscing about all of the famous train routes he had taken worldwide and the many he hoped to travel one day.

His penchant for walking may have made Swain a legend in Boron and the surrounding area, but it was the man himself who earned the love of the town proper. As stated, Swain would always help those in need, but he could also be found every Sunday playing the organ or piano in either the First Baptist Church of Boron or Saint Joseph's Catholic Church. Swain joked that he was a "church-going atheist." He also helped out the Boron High School drama department a couple of times by playing the music

George Swain is a legend in the town of Boron and surrounding area not in small part to his size 14 boots.

for its presentations of Gilbert and Sullivan's *H.M.S. Pinafore* and *Trial by Jury*. Walking George also took it upon himself to teach piano and music to children in the community.

In 1978, the exploits of Walking George came to the attention of a television production team (some believe that townsfolk tipped them off), and in 1979, the TV show *Real People* profiled George for one of its episodes. Walking George Swain has also had his story told in the *Los Angeles Times* and other newspapers.

George Swain passed away on April 25, 2000. He was eighty years old when he was found dead from an irregular heartbeat on the porch of a neighbor's home, where he was house-sitting. When Boron heard the news, the entire town wept. Boron had lost a true gentleman, a friend to all and a man who loved them all back. The way people felt about Walking George Swain was summed up best by Pat Mosley from the John Muir Memorial

Association newsletter, *The View from John Muir's Window*: "George was truly a character and those of us that knew him can only say it was a pleasure to have known him and all the joy he brought to our ordinary lives."

To learn more about George Swain, visit the Twenty Mule Team Museum in the town of Boron, California. There, you can view photos of Walking George and see his size 14EEE boots.

2

PANCHO BARNES

Another interesting character who spent their last years in the town of Boron is aviation legend Pancho Barnes. Although not as famous as her contemporary, Amelia Earhart, Barnes had a much more interesting and longer life than Earhart. Born Florence Leontine Lowe, Barnes grew up the daughter of a man who always treated her like the son he always wanted, which suited the tomboy quite nicely. Barnes did have a brother, William Emmert, but the child was always sickly and passed away when Barnes was only twelve years old.

Florence was truly a tomboy growing up. Her parents were well off, but she wanted nothing to do with the wealthy lifestyle and conformity that money entailed. As such, she repeatedly ran away from home during her teen years, once even riding her horse down to Tijuana before her parents placed her in a boarding school in the town of La Jolla, California. Somehow, she managed to make it through the last two years before graduating. After finishing school, she told her mother and father that she wanted to be a veterinarian. Her mother vehemently objected and enrolled her in art school, which, according to her mother, was a more "ladylike" education. Her grandmother, going one step further, arranged a marriage for Florence to Episcopalian reverend C. Rankin Barnes. So, at the young age of nineteen, Florence became the wife of a man she didn't love, didn't know and didn't really want to know. The first time they kissed was at the wedding, and the only time they were intimate was the night of the honeymoon. As luck would have it, nine months later, Florence gave birth to a son, William Emmert Barnes, or "Billy" for short.

Pancho Barnes loved nothing more than a good time. It was hard to find her without her trademark, infectious smile. *Courtesy of Colonel Vernon P. Saxon Jr. Aerospace Museum.*

Barnes had no maternal instinct whatsoever. Shortly after her mother passed away less than three years later, Florence up and left. In the next few years, Florence traveled the country, had a couple of affairs and thoroughly enjoyed her freedom. She also made a trip to South America and partied with her companions the entire time. Of the trip, she said: "Ah hell. We had more fun in a week than those weenies [her wealthy peers] had in a lifetime."

Once back in the States, Barnes told tales of her exploits, which caused her compatriots to suggest a trip back to South America by working on a banana boat. Barnes jumped at the chance. So, disguised as a man, she hired on a boat heading south for yet another adventure. Shortly after leaving port, however, the crew found out that what they were actually doing was smuggling guns and ammunition into Mexico to aid revolutionaries fighting the Mexican government. As soon as the boat reached its destination, the boat was boarded and the entire crew held hostage.

For six weeks, Barnes was locked up. Never one to play it safe, she found another crew member, helmsman Roger Chute, who was brave enough to try to escape, and that is exactly what they did. The two stole a horse and a burro and headed out from Mexico City to Veracruz. On the long trek, Barnes looked over at Chute riding his horse and joked that he looked just like Don Quixote. Chute responded with, "Well, if I'm Quixote, that must mean you're Pancho!" Barnes tried to correct Chute, telling him that the sidekick was named Sancho Panza but Chute said he liked the name *Pancho* better. After thinking about it for a few minutes, Barnes agreed, and the name stuck.

After stowing away on a boat in Veracruz, the two made it back to the United States, and Pancho Barnes spent the next two years partying and having fun with the large inheritance she received from a rich relative. Barnes found that she needed something more, something exciting to do. While driving her cousin to his flight lessons, she reminisced on the time her grandfather had taken her to an airshow when she was ten years old. She remembered how exhilarating it had been and how thrilling it was to watch the loops and dives and barrel rolls. Barnes signed up for flight lessons after dropping off her cousin.

Florence "Pancho" Barnes, was as skilled, if not more so than her friend and colleague Amelia Earhart. *Courtesy of Colonel Vernon P. Saxon Jr. Aerospace Museum.*

Pancho Barnes soloed after only six hours of instruction, bought herself a biplane and immediately started barnstorming. Even after she crashed her airplane in 1929, Barnes jumped right back into the cockpit. She was sponsored by Union Oil. Barnes broke Amelia Earhart's women's world speed record with an average sustained speed of 196.19 miles per hour. When Union Oil's sponsorship ended, Barnes headed to Hollywood.

In Tinsel Town, Pancho became a stunt pilot. Her first gig was to provide authentic airplane sounds for Howard Hugh's Academy Award–winning movie *Hell's Angels*. During 1930, Barnes worked on several adventure films, providing aerial stunts and exciting airplane footage. In 1931, she started the Associated Motion Picture Pilots group, one of Hollywood's first unions. She also organized the Women's Air Reserve, dedicated to bringing attention to the need for equal qualifications for aviatrixes and to encourage more women to pursue aviation as a career.

While Pancho was flying, and organizing, her hard-partying lifestyle remained unchanged. With all of the food, booze and sundry items needed to supply a steady guest list at her mansion, Barnes finally ran out of money in 1935. She had to sell her family's San Marino mansion and traded her Los Angeles apartment for an alfalfa ranch near Muroc Dry Lake in Antelope Valley, California. She named her new estate Rancho Oro Verde. The nearest town was twenty miles away, but there was a U.S. Army Air Corps field nearby, and this gave Barnes an idea.

Not knowing how to farm alfalfa, Pancho bought some pigs and dairy cows and opened up her home to the local flyboys. The commanding officer of the Flight Test Center, Colonel Clarence Shoop, used Pancho's facilities to host parties for his guests and for visiting dignitaries, all for a price, of course. In 1935, the Civilian Pilot Training Program was established to train pilots for the military, and Barnes, never one to let an opportunity slip by, secured a government contract to provide the planes and the instructors for the program. One of the students caught Pancho's eye, and it wasn't long before Nicky Hudson became Barnes's second husband—well, for two weeks at least.

When the Japanese bombed Pearl Harbor, the training program was ended. Muroc Army Air Field became Edwards Air Force Base, and the population of the area skyrocketed as men and their families came to stay near the base. Barnes of course took advantage of the influx and expanded her business, serving the guys from the base good meals and entertainment. Even her Hollywood friends came out to join the fun. In 1944, Barnes married her third husband. This marriage lasted four months, a new personal record for Pancho.

After World War II ended, Pancho began improving her property, expanded her airfield and called the whole thing Pancho's Fly-Inn. Anybody could fly in for free, but they had to purchase their gas and oil from her as compensation. Barnes eventually added a repair shop, hangars and a flight school to the airport. She added extra rooms, as well as air-conditioning and private baths to the guest house. She also added a race track. Barnes advertised the facility as a "modern flying dude ranch." She charged forty-nine dollars a week per person, which included meals. Her establishment was growing popular with high-ranking military officers such as General Henry "Hap" Arnold, Edwards Air Force Base commanding officer Al Boyd, her old friend General Jimmy Doolittle and even Chuck Yeager. Because of the high-profile guests and constant crowd coming and going, Barnes reinvented her resort and called it the Happy Bottom Riding Club. The walls of her new bar were soon covered with photographs of pilots and their aircraft, including prototypes. Many of the photos were autographed by the pilots themselves. The Happy Bottom Riding Club in this iteration was the inspiration for the bar in the 1984 movie *The Right Stuff*.

In 1946, Barnes began suffering from hypertension. Even though her doctors told her she needed to cut back on her drinking, Barnes wouldn't do it. She eventually developed a retinal hemorrhage but flat-out refused treatment. When Pancho finally collapsed in her club, the decision was made for her, and she underwent an experimental treatment that required two separate surgeries. During her recovery, a pilot by the name of Eugene "Mac" McKendry, who had recently moved onto the ranch, stayed by Pancho's side the whole time. By 1952, Barnes was planning her fourth wedding, this time to McKendry.

Edwards Air Force Base commander Al Boyd gave Pancho away; Chuck Yeager stood as her attendant. When the judge finished the ceremony, the 650 attendees gave a raucous cheer, headed over to Barnes's second ceremony— this one a traditional Native American wedding—and then proceeded to the feast, which included four roasted pigs, eighty pounds of potato salad,

The Happy Bottom Riding Club was where most of the pilots of Edwards Air Force Base would hang out. Here, Pancho has some fun with her guests. Some of America's most famous aviators passed through the club's doors. *Courtesy of Colonel Vernon P. Saxon Jr. Aerospace Museum.*

sixteen gallons of Jell-O (flavor not mentioned) and a fifty-pound wedding cake. Naturally, the booze flowed freely for all in attendance.

Shortly after the wedding, Edwards saw a change in command. Boyd was replaced as commanding officer by General Stanley Holtoner. The new commander was strictly by the book and wasn't at all amused by the goings-on at the Happy Bottom Riding Club. Holtoner accused Barnes of running a brothel and declared the club off-limits to all military personnel, seriously curtailing Barnes's profits. The air force was also buying up land around Edwards for a runway expansion and were lowballing Barnes in an effort to force her off of her property. She, of course, fought them all the way, which didn't sit well with Holtoner. Then, mysteriously, while driving home from shopping, Barnes saw smoke coming from her place and realized that it was already fully engulfed in flames and was a total loss. Pancho was still fighting the government to get her name cleared and to get it to back off on the sale of her property. But after the fire destroyed everything she owned, Barnes finally settled for $375,000 and her name made whole. There is still suspicion surrounding the cause of the fire; the blaze itself was portrayed in the 1984 film, albeit with a bit of skewing of the timeline. After all of the threats, the dragging of Barnes's name through the mud and the dubious nature of the fire, the U.S. Air Force never built the proposed new runway.

As the 1960s dawned, Pancho's marriage was falling apart, and in 1962, she filed for divorce from Mac. With her health failing, Barnes moved into a friend's tiny twenty-by-twenty-five-square-foot house and began breeding Yorkshire terriers. Barnes also began speaking at local clubs, banquets and other events as a way of bringing in much-needed cash. In the summer of 1971, a few of Barnes's old friends from Edwards Air Force Base threw a party for her seventieth birthday, Buzz Aldrin chief among the attendees. The party in her honor was held at Edwards, near her old club.

On March 30, 1975, a friend phoned Pancho but couldn't get in touch with her. When Barnes failed to show up to speak at the annual Barnstormers Reunion on April 5, her son went looking for her. When he arrived at her small home, he found the place in squalid conditions. Trash and animal feces covered the floor, and in the middle of it all was the body of his mother.

Pancho Barnes passed away at her house in Boron, California. I was told that the real truth of her death was more gruesome than is known publicly.

Barnes had obviously been dead for a few days. It seemed that the cancer his mother had been suffering from had finally won the battle.

Her son, Billy, had his mother cremated and received permission from the air force to scatter her ashes over her old stomping grounds. The Cessna flew low over the area, and a friend carefully began spreading Barnes's ashes over what used to be the Happy Bottom Riding Club. As the ashes drifted down, a crosswind rose and carried the ashes back into the cockpit of the small plane. It would seem that even in death Pancho was not ready to give up her passion for flying.

3

LEMOYNE HAZARD, RED FISH AND RAPSCALLIONS

Born in Los Angeles, California, on January 12, 1880, Lemoyne Anthony Hazard was one of those rare individuals who had a way with people. He had a calm demeanor that transferred itself to others just by being around him. Lemoyne also liked to help people, not by giving them handouts—although I'm sure he did that often—but by giving them knowledge, making sure that they were safe and knowing where they were going. Hazard also didn't mind using this personable connection to help in his business endeavors.

After marrying his sweetheart, Ida Bell, in 1908, Hazard moved to the small town of Bishop in the Owens Valley. With automobiles becoming cheap enough and more available, America was discovering the joys of driving along the country's open, mostly dirt, roads. When, in 1909, the state legislature called for an $18 million bond to construct the State Highway System, Inyo County, following the national Good Roads movement, established its own version, the Inyo Goods Roads Club. The club started out with sixty-two members, and when Hazard moved to Inyo, he joined the club. Hazard decided that with the country experiencing the freedom of the road, and with the promotion of the proposed El Camino Sierra route, travelers were going to need repairs on their newfangled automobiles. To this end, Hazard built one of the first auto-repair shops in Inyo County.

Hazard's Garage, at Main Street (Highway 395) and Lagoon Street, was visible from the road, but to draw attention to it, Hazard erected a giant, wooden red fish with the word *Hazard's* painted in bold letters on both sides.

Lemoyne Hazard loved cars. Here, we see Lemoyne behind the wheel out for a drive with a friend along the El Camino Sierra. (Note the Red Fish on the front engine cowling.) *Courtesy of Eastern California Museum.*

As more motorists drove to see the sights in the valley and surrounding mountains, repair work grew. One of the things Lemoyne noticed was that travelers were constantly asking for directions, where the best spots to see the natural beauty of the Sierra were located and where they could stay to either camp or lodge. Hazard began to realize that if motorists were given as much information as possible while traveling along the new, developing roadways, not only could it bring more travelers to the Eastern Sierra, but it also could generate more business for himself and the other establishments along the El Camino Sierra. To this end, Hazard came up with a brilliant idea that would accomplish both tasks: the Red Fish.

Using the giant symbol of the red fish featured in advertising for his auto-repair shop, Hazard began creating more red fish. Now, however, instead of advertising his garage, Hazard painted town names and mileages large enough for motorists to see as they drove past. From Mojave to Lake Tahoe, and along Highway 6 from Bishop to Utah, Hazard placed hundreds of red fish signs to help travelers find their way to the Owens Valley and Inyo

County. Over time, these red fish direction signs became as familiar to motorists as the Burma Shave signs would become on American roadways. Even though Hazard had never officially named the signs, they became known as the Red Fish.

Even though Hazard was giving travelers directions to towns along the way, it still didn't stop them from asking about the different sites and sightseeing in the area. Again, Hazard came up with a way to help out not only the travelers but also the businesses along the route. Lemoyne, always fond of the written word, created a travel guide called *Dreamalog*. This guide not only told explorers of the highway where they could find the natural beauty along the El Camino Sierra and where to camp and lodge, but he also included detailed maps of the areas they would be traveling through. Not only were there maps, stories and locations in the guides for the enjoyment of motorists but also advertisements for businesses up and down the Owens Valley, helping to bring prominence and economic aid to the area. Hazard himself published and then distributed these guides to tourist locations from Mojave to Lake Tahoe and along Highway 6. With the Red Fish becoming so well known around the country, other people began designing and using similar fish signs to promote their business. It

The Red Fish may be gone from our memories, much like the Burma Shave signs, but you can still see these icons of days gone by at the Laws Museum in Bishop, California.

became so widespread that Hazard eventually was forced to copyright the Red Fish to put a stop to it.

So popular and successful were the Red Fish that those driving through Bishop immediately noticed the original sign that hung over Hazard's Garage. People would stop by just to chat about their trip, ask about the many signs along the way and stop in so they could say that they had been to the Red Fish itself. Lemoyne Hazard, still a businessman, used the newfound popularity to his advantage. With so many people coming in to say hello, Hazard expanded his garage and became a dealership for Dodge Brothers cars. As this dealership began to grow and become a success, he once more expanded and added a Buick dealership. Life, and Inyo County, were being good to Lemoyne Hazard.

Hazard was many things, but ungrateful wasn't one of them. With his success and his prominence in Inyo County and Owens Valley growing, he wanted to give back to the community that had been so good to him. He joined the Inyo County Sheriff Department. Hazard had always been good with people, and this ability came in handy with his duties as a deputy sheriff. Many times, Hazard was able to defuse dangerous or hostile situations simply by talking and using his calming presence. Many in Inyo came to respect Hazard not only for his promotion of the economic health of the region but also for his dedication to the safety and peace of those he served. Unfortunately, not all people can be subdued with kind words and reason, especially when the one needing to be calmed down has been drinking.

While on duty on January 12, 1925, just one day before Lemoyne Hazard's forty-sixth birthday, he and his partner, Deputy W. Rathjen, were called to a domestic disturbance in Laws, California. They were joined at the residence by Indian Agent R. Pratt from the nearby Indian camp, and together the three officers approached the house of Charlie Jackson and family. The call had been for spousal abuse, so the three men proceeded with extreme caution. Before the officers could reach the door, Jackson, described by the *Santa Ana Register* on January 23, 1925, as a "whiskey-crazed Indian," appeared on the porch holding a shotgun. Jackson immediately began firing on the officers, hitting all three men. Hazard was seriously wounded, and the other two men sought shelter from the gunfire. Jackson approached Hazard and began using the butt end of the shotgun to repeatedly strike Hazard about the head. A shootout began, and Jackson was apprehended after he ran out of shells for his weapon. Hazard had been beaten so badly that the stock on the gun shattered. Lemoyne Hazard was dead by the time the short gun battle ended. A coroner's report

Lemoyne Hazard was deadly serious in upholding the law. Here, we see Lemoyne shortly before he was killed in the line of duty by a drunken man. *Courtesy of Eastern California Museum.*

It was on this corner at Lagoon and Main (395) Streets, that Hazard's Garage served travelers along Highway 395.

said that the cause of death was from the blows to his head and not the gunshot wound. Charlie Jackson was sentenced to life in prison and sent to San Quentin.

After Hazard's death, his family not only continued promoting the area and the Red Fish but also expanded the Red Fish campaign by handing out decals advertising Bishop and their business. They eventually sold the garage and dealerships and moved back to Southern California. Those who purchased the business ran it for just a few years before they sold the property and left the area. With Hazard gone and his family moving, the Red Fish began to disappear. When the National Beautify America project was established by Lady Bird Johnson, many of Hazard's signs were removed by collectors until the Red Fish were nothing more than a memory of days gone by, much like the Burma Shave signs they were compared to.

Today, the building where Lemoyne Hazard set up his garage and dealership is still there, as is the house he built by hand. It still stands just off Line Street. Many businesses still use the Red Fish symbol, but all of the signs that Hazard so carefully erected are now gone from the roadways. Luckily, the Laws Museum, just outside of Bishop on Route 6, saved two of these iconic signs, which are on display for all to see.

Today, Lemoyne Hazard is not well known, if he is known at all. But he was a true pioneer of the Owens Valley and Inyo County and was one of the true gentlemen who graced the Sierra.

4

NORMAN CLYDE

No book about the legends and lore of Highway 395 would be complete without the story of one of the most prolific climbers and mountaineers who ever walked the Sierra Mountains. I am talking about Norman Clyde. Someone who only other explorers, climbers, avid hikers and adventure seekers would know about, Clyde saved scores of people, found the bodies of climbers when everyone else had given up and had more first climbs than almost anyone in history. Clyde certainly fits the bill of legend when it comes to the Eastern Sierra Range.

Norman was born on April 8, 1885, in Philadelphia and lived most of his early life far from the mountains and peaks that would become his true passion. After high school, Norman graduated from Geneva College with a degree in classical literature with the idea of becoming a teacher. He took on numerous jobs in education, including one in Fargo, North Dakota, and another in Mount Pleasant, Utah, before returning to school in 1911, attending the University of California–Berkeley. After he completed his graduate studies, Norman Clyde went back to teaching. This time, however, he stayed in California.

While attending school and teaching in Northern California, Norman discovered the joys of hiking the pristine mountain trails, fishing in the clear lakes and even climbing some of the smaller cliff faces he found while communing with nature. At this time in his life, mountaineering was nothing more than a hobby, a way for him to relax and unwind from the rigors of dealing with the kids he taught. It was in 1914 that Norman found the fledgling Sierra Club, joining the group a year later. The facts of Clyde's life over the next few years are relatively unknown, as he was not predisposed to talk about them. It was both one of the best and one of the worst times in Norman Clyde's life.

Clyde met a pretty young woman by the name of Winifred May Bolster, a nurse at a tuberculosis hospital. The two were married on June 15, 1915, in Pasadena, California, and couldn't have been happier. It is not known whether Clyde took a teaching job near his wife's hospital, but we do know that only a few short years after their marriage, Winifred contracted the deadly disease herself. After suffering for a couple of years, Norman's wife passed away. This tragedy would be the catalyst for the change in Norman Clyde's life.

After the death of his wife, Norman Clyde moved to the Eastern Sierra town of Independence, California. Clyde took a job as a teacher and principal of the high school. While working there, Clyde renewed his trips into the local mountains and found that hiking in the backcountry and climbing the rugged peaks and trails of the Sierra offered him a peace he hadn't been able to find since before Winifred's death. His job at the high school was short-lived. After witnessing four years of Halloween pranks that vandalized the school, in 1927, Clyde decided to end the antics. During a confrontation with a group of students, Clyde fired a couple of pistol rounds into the air. One round struck a car carrying eight students. Although no one was injured in the incident, that spelled the end of Clyde's educational career.

After he resigned from the school, Norman took up writing about his exploits climbing in the Eastern Sierra. He had been leading youths into the mountains since he arrived in Independence and had been making solo climbs of the many peaks and minarets (the jagged peaks located in the Ritter Range of the Sierra Nevada Mountains). In 1925 alone, Clyde recorded forty-eight climbs, half of which were "first ascents"—that is, Norman Clyde was the first human to attempt and succeed in climbing these peaks. By the following year, he had recorded sixty climbs, more than even the renowned Ansel Adams had achieved. Being a freelance author was not paying Clyde's bills, however. To make extra money, Clyde offered his services as a mountain guide, leading experienced mountaineers, including United States Geological Survey (USGS) surveyors, as well as novice climbers to some of the most challenging summits in the Sierra. During the winter months, Norman acted as caretaker to some of the lodges in the area, such as Giant Forest at Sequoia, Glacier Lodge outside of Big Pine and Glacier

Norman Clyde was not only famous for being perhaps the best mountaineer in history but also for his exceptionally large backpack. *Courtesy of Eastern California Museum.*

Point at Yosemite. Norman even hired on a few seasons as the caretaker for Hollywood actor Lon Chaney Sr.'s fishing cabin.

During this time, Clyde was earning a reputation as an expert mountaineer and climber. Rangers came to Clyde to ask for help locating downed aircraft or missing hikers and, if need be, to recover bodies. In one amazing incident, after everyone else had given up looking for a well-respected climber, Clyde refused to give up the search and found the man's body. It may not have been the outcome everyone had hoped for, but it did allow closure for the family.

Peter Starr was one of the best mountaineers in the country. He had scaled over forty of the world's most challenging summits and was working on a guidebook to survey and inform interested hikers on the newly completed John Muir Trail. Starr loved the mountains and loved climbing and spent most of his time away from work in mountaineering activities. In July 1933, Peter Starr went missing in his beloved Sierra Mountains.

As a member of the Sierra Club, Starr was a well-respected and admired climber. When it was made known that he was missing during a climb, club president Francis Farquhar, using a biplane, crisscrossed the area where Starr had been climbing but found no sign of the missing mountaineer. (This is said to be the first aerial search in Sierra history.) Farquhar then gathered the best climbers and mountaineers he could find to begin a ground search for the missing man. One of these was Norman Clyde.

As mentioned, Clyde rivaled or exceeded John Muir for the title of foremost Sierra mountaineer. Muir may have done more to preserve the range through his lectures, writings and documentation, but Clyde's exploits are unsurpassed to this day. Norman Clyde was the first to scale what is now named Clyde Minaret, the tallest peak in its chain at 12,281 feet. And by the time of this search and rescue, he had recorded eighty-two first ascents in the Sierra. (Some figures have Clyde's total as high as one thousand during his lifetime.)

When Clyde got the message that he was needed, he was climbing a glacier with his friend Oliver Kerhlein. It took the two men only a few hours to reach the base camp set up for the rescue operation near Lake Ediza. Even though there had never been a doubt about Norman Clyde joining the search, when Clyde found out who was missing, he grew even more determined to find the man. Even though Starr and Clyde had never met, they had a deep admiration for each other. Starr mentioned the other mountaineer in his guidebook, about how Clyde was the only man to climb North Palisades by the hardest route possible: "It is amusing to compare Clyde's brief and modest account of the very difficult ascent appearing in the register with the lengthy and exhilarated accounts of some of the parties who made the ascent by the route I have described." Clyde, on the other hand, respected Starr for his abilities as an expert mountaineer and for trying through his guidebook to bring the beauty of the Sierra to those who may not have known about them.

The search was broken up into the most likely areas where Starr was thought to have been climbing; four teams of two men each were formed to locate Starr. Clues were found and Starr's camp was located, but no sign of the man himself was found. A few days into looking for Starr, and with fading hope of finding his son alive, Walter Starr called off the search, gathered his son's belongings that had been left at his camp and headed home to break the terrible news to his wife. The other mountaineers packed up and left camp, all with the sobering knowledge that they had lost a mountaineering brother and friend. As the last of the search party left camp, Norman Clyde looked up at the peaks and refused to give up searching for the man who had earned his respect.

For five more days, Norman Clyde, alone, climbed routes in and around the peaks. He was looking for any sign he could find—cigarette butts, trash, bits of torn cloth, anything that might lead him to the lost climber. Clyde was not the sort of man to give up, but he now knew that if and when he found Starr, the man would most likely not be alive. Starr had been too long in the elements. The search had now become a body recovery.

Clyde stood in camp one evening looking up at the mountains before him. He glanced over to Michael Minaret and realized that it was the last possible place to look. It had already been checked twice by other teams, which is why he hadn't looked there himself. One team had found a partial cigarette of the brand Starr smoked, and there was no register entry by Starr at the peak, so Clyde figured he better have a look. The next morning, he began his ascent of Michael Minaret. He scaled the almost ninety-degree face of the rock and reached the summit by midday. After writing his name in the register, he stood looking out over the landscape, wondering where on earth Starr could be. After a brief rest, Clyde began his descent. On the way down, he made a discovery that has placed him in the annals of legends of the Sierra. This is how Norman Clyde explains the encounter.

> *As I carefully and deliberately made my way down toward the notch, I scanned and re-scanned the northwestern face. Much of it was concealed by irregularities. Suddenly a fly droned past, then another, and another....I began to follow a ledge running in a northwesterly direction. When I had gone along it but a few yards, turning about, I looked upward and across the chute to the northwestern face. There, lying on the ledge not more than fifty yards distant, were the earthly remains of Walter A. Starr Jr. He had obviously fallen, perhaps several hundred feet, to instantaneous death.*

Clyde somberly made his way down the mountain and caught a ride to Mammoth Lakes, where he sent a telegram to the Starr household. Word that their son's remains had been found reached the family the following day.

On August 30, 1933, Norman Clyde and Jules Eichorn, dressed in black, made the dangerous climb back up to where Starr fell. There, they carefully placed Starr's body into a canvas sack and placed a cairn over the young man, giving him a proper burial. The grave is still there today and, at twelve thousand feet, is the highest known resting place in the Sierra and perhaps the country.

A couple of weeks after her son was buried, Carmen Starr wrote to Norman: "I know of no words adequate in which to express to you the gratitude I feel for your great efforts which finally resulted in your finding our beloved boy. The knowledge of what had been his actual fate lifted our hearts, a burden that I do not see how we could have lived under." In thanks for both Clyde's determination in finding her son and in appreciation for both Clyde and Eichorn going back to tend to Peter's remains, the Starrs gave Clyde a stipend for the rest of his life and paid for Eichorn to attend UC-Berkeley, where he graduated with a degree in music. Using his son's notes, Starr's father completed Peter's guidebook in 1934. It is still in print.

Norman Clyde was not a large man by any stretch of the imagination. He weighed only 140 pounds, but that didn't stop him from making sure he always had what he needed stuffed somewhere in his pack. Although not much is known about the man himself, his backpacks became the stuff of legend. Clyde would lead many Sierra Club trips and earned a nickname among the club's members: "The Pack That Walks Like a Man." Norman Clyde's packs were huge. He would routinely carry five cameras, a full-length Hudson Bay axe, cups, spoons, other utensils, dishes and bowls, six large kettles, salt and pepper shakers, condiments, graters and several sets of boots—ski, rubber-soled, camp slippers, snow boots. He also carried a hammer and a small cobbler's anvil (he often denied that he carried the anvil) to make repairs to his and his clients' shoes if necessary. And, of course, he carried his books. Clyde loved to read. His packs routinely weighed about 75 pounds. One of Clyde's friends, Robert Underhill, once said of the man's packs, "They were an especially picturesque enormity of skyscraper architecture."

There is a story that on one of his climbs, Clyde spent the night in a surveyor's camp. The following morning, the other men, who had marveled at the sight of his huge backpack, decided to play a prank on Norman. As they prepared to break camp, the surveyors began explaining the dangers of running out of food in the wilderness. One by one, each man offered Norman a few cans of food and other items that could "help save his life" if he was caught unawares. Clyde, never one to turn down free food and gear, smiled, nodded and gratefully accepted the offered items. As the men parted ways, the surveyors laughed at the "greenie" they thought Clyde to be, and Clyde grinned as he made his way down the mountain with his haul of new supplies. His pack now weighed about ninety-five pounds. Norman, of course, didn't mind.

Norman Clyde's legacy stands for all who would look. Clyde Minaret, Clyde's Ledge, Clyde's Meadow on Mount Whitney itself and, of course, Norman Clyde Peak, all bear his name. How many hikers and lost climbers Norman Clyde saved is lost to time, as are those deceased he recovered. His record for first ascents is unmatched today. Clyde's accomplishments are best summed up in the 1947 *Sierra Club Handbook*.

> *Outstanding among members who have helped others gain mountain experience is Norman Clyde, whose amazing achievements in scaling practically all the peaks in the High Sierra are well known to mountaineers. More than one climber has exulted in a supposedly first ascent, only to find later that Clyde went up that "unclimbed peak" in the winter of, say, 1920! There are many seasoned climbers who can look back on their early days as novices in the mountains and remember with gratitude what they learned from Clyde.*

It is plain to see how Norman Clyde became a legend along Highway 395. It would be an understatement to say that Clyde felt more at home in the

Not even heavy snow could keep Norman Clyde from an ascent or looking for lost and missing climbers. *Courtesy of Eastern California Museum.*

mountains and on the peaks of the Sierra than anywhere else. He spent his life exploring them, leading others into their majesty and creating a legend of himself, albeit unintentionally, that no one as yet has lived up to. In 1966, at the age of seventy-six, he was still spending his summers acting as a guide on Sierra Club base camp trips. Unfortunately, his age brought him down to live in the small town of Big Pine, but his trips leading private parties into his beloved Sierra continued until he was diagnosed with cancer in his left eye. In 1968, he was transferred to a nursing home in Bishop, California, where his eye was removed a year later. Norman Clyde died in 1972 at the age of eighty-seven surrounded by his beloved Sierra peaks. After Clyde's funeral, his friends, Smoke Blanchard and Blanchard's son, along with a party of admirers and Clyde's close lifelong friend Jules Eichorn, took Norman up to the peak that bears his name and scattered his ashes so that he could spend eternity on the mountains he called home.

5

GEORGE W.G. FERRIS

Although a product not of California but of nearby Carson City, the capital of Nevada, George Ferris deserves a mention in any book dealing with US 395. It all began in 1859, when Ferris was just five years old and his family moved from Illinois to Genoa, Nevada. Along the way, the Ferris family had to cross the Carson River, and there, young George saw a waterwheel turning in the river that helped irrigate the crops and fields nearby. Ferris didn't care what the wheel was used for, but its image stuck with him through school in Carson City, in his university days in California and into his engineering career and the forming of his business, analyzing structural steel and metals.

In 1889, when Gustave Eiffel unveiled his 984-foot-tall tower for the Universal Exposition, the world marveled at the engineering masterpiece of the wrought-iron latticework and was amazed that something like it could be built. Eiffel's tower was being compared to Saint Peter's Cathedral in Rome and the Great Pyramids in Egypt. The sheer splendor of the structure not only caused a stir of appreciation throughout the world, but it also left the United States with a quandary. You see, the United States, namely Chicago, was set to host the 1893 World's Columbian Exposition. As France had just set the standard for all subsequent expositions, the man tasked with turning a square mile of Chicago landscape into a dazzling world showpiece, Daniel Burnham, was at a loss as to how he would match the spectacle of the Eiffel Tower.

Burnham gathered a group of engineers who were already working on the project to come up with "something novel, original, daring and unique." The engineers began to toss ideas Burnham's way: a tower built with rails leading to distant cities that would allow visitors to toboggan home; small cars atop a tower that could be pushed off the edge in an early example of bungee jumping; even a replica of the Eiffel Tower, only bigger and taller. None of these ideas would convey the message Burnham wanted to send to the world, that America was, in its own right, an engineering powerhouse and ready for the world stage.

George Ferris was a member of the team who sat in on the meeting, and he took what Burnham said as a challenge. As the ideas kept coming in and were being rejected, Ferris was thinking about what the world might find not only impressive but also memorable. The Eiffel Tower was just that, a tower. The recently erected Statue of Liberty was only a statue. They were both impressive in their own right, but both were of a mundane nature. As Ferris thought, his mind kept coming back to the waterwheel he had seen as a child and had visited many times while living in Carson City. As he thought about it, he saw the wheel built not of wood but of metal, and instead of paddles that picked up and carried water, the wheel was fitted with gondolas that could pick up and carry people. George began to design this wheel, using his expertise in metallurgy as his foundation. When he was ready, he pitched his idea to Burnham and the rest of the group.

At first, Burnham and the other engineers laughed at his idea. A carpenter, William Somers, was building similar wheels at Asbury Park, but his were only 50 feet tall and made of thick lumber. What Ferris was proposing was a 250-foot-tall monstrosity that carried thirty-six gondolas that could carry sixty people each, each made of thin metal rods. Burnham and the engineers told Ferris that his wheel would be too fragile to be safe. Undeterred, Ferris hired engineers to assess and check his calculations, paid for safety studies and brought in investors, all to make sure his design was not only feasible but also safe. All told, Ferris spent about $25,000 of his own money to make sure it would work. When all of the studies were complete and proof was in hand, Ferris returned to Burnham and the others with his findings. Impressed with his work, Burnham gave him the contract and the go-ahead to build his Ferris wheel.

Work began on the Ferris wheel almost immediately. The contraption was built with more than 100,000 parts. It had a main wheel that rose to a height of 264 feet, spinning around a central axle that weighed almost 45 tons and was fitted onto two towers that were 140 feet high. The thirty-six gondolas were fitted with revolving seats that allowed riders a spectacular view of Chicago and the surrounding countryside. The ride itself cost fifty cents and lasted twenty minutes with two full rotations. One rotation allowed each gondola to be loaded and off-loaded, with one full, nonstop, nine-minute rotation on each ride. Each passenger was afforded a stop at the top of the arc to take in the view. The Observation Wheel, as it was officially known, was so popular that in just under five months the wheel had seen almost two million people take the thrilling ride on Ferris's marvelous invention.

After the World's Columbian Exposition in Chicago closed its gates, Ferris's debtors came looking for what he owed them. Ferris had intended to pay his debts using the money owed him by the fair promoters but found that they had not lived up to their agreement—at least he believed they hadn't—and had failed to pay him what was owed. As the collections and lawsuits began to accumulate, Ferris was forced to sue the fair. His troubles began to pile up in the interim. Replicas of his Ferris wheel began to pop up all around the country in amusement parks and seaside piers. Coney Island, in New York, had more than one built and began advertising the wheel as its creation. Since Ferris was tied up in wheel-related legal matters and hadn't had time to patent his invention, there wasn't much he could do to stop the copying of his observation wheel. Ferris ended up losing his court case against the fair promoters and eventually ended up bankrupt as a result of his debts. Ferris died in November 1896 at the age of thirty-seven, broke and suffering from typhoid, only a few months after his wife left him.

As for the observation wheel, after the Chicago exposition closed, the wheel was dismantled and stored for a few years before being sold to the 1904 Louisiana Purchase Exposition in St. Louis. The wheel had as much success at this exposition as it had in Chicago. However, once this exposition was over, and with so many replicas now in operation, the need for the original massive observation wheel had diminished. Two years after the St. Louis fair ended, the wheel was sold to a wrecker. The metal from the original Farris wheel was used in the construction of the navy vessel USS *Illinois* for use in World War I.

Although the Observation Wheel was never officially called a Ferris Wheel, the name *Ferris* has now become synonymous with the ride known all around the world. If not for the chance encounter of a boy with a waterwheel on the Carson River along what is now US Highway 395, one wonders if the ride we all know from our summer country fairs and carnivals would exist at all. It would be a much drearier world without the Ferris Wheel to add its touch of romance to date night in America.

6

NELLIE BLY BAKER

M any people may know about Nellie Bly the reporter, her around-the-world adventure, suffrage and her investigative journalism. But few if any know about Nellie Bly Baker. Although not as well known, Baker was herself famous for a time, as adventurous as reporter Bly and in so many ways more capable. Movie star, trendsetter, mountain guide, lodge host and visionary, Nellie Bly Baker deserves a spot next to Nellie Bly the journalist in the historical annals of the United States.

Nellie Bly Baker was born in the Oklahoma Territory in 1893 in present-day Yukon Township but was raised in Wagoner County. Nellie loved the outdoors, and her older brothers taught her how to hunt, fish, ride and handle firearms. She seemed to have a natural way with animals, both domestic and wild. Growing up, Nellie never seemed to want to do the things other girls her age enjoyed, and her adventurous spirit seemed to dominate her life. Her parents began to worry that she would never attract a suitable husband with her freedom-loving lifestyle and sent her away to a convent in the hopes that it would settle her down. Of course, convent life was not for Nellie. After two years, without having been slowed down a bit, she left the nuns to get an actual education.

Nellie enrolled in college, received a business degree and took a job in Tulsa as a stenographer. When, in 1918, Nellie's sister Ollie May announced that she was moving to Hollywood, Nellie, bored with her job, decided to move with her. Once there, Nellie and her sister took odd jobs in various studios, and Nellie decided to attend the California School for Movie

Nellie Bly Baker was a woman before her time. Movie star, adventurer, mountain guide and more. Truly an extraordinary woman. *Courtesy of Mono Basin Historical Society.*

Operators. Nellie Bly Baker became the first woman in history to be licensed as a motion-picture projectionist. She worked this job for a couple of years and then took a job as a secretary at First National Pictures, where Charlie Chaplin produced his films before starting his own studio.

Chaplin immediately noticed Nellie's natural beauty and, after talking with her on many occasions, realized that she seemed to have a natural talent for acting. Chaplin cast Nellie in her first film in 1921, *The Kid*, and again in 1923 in *A Woman in Paris*, both uncredited for Baker. Her presence in *A Woman in Paris* caught the eye of producer-director Constance Talmadge, who cast Nellie in *The Goldfish*, and from there Nellie Baker's career took off. Nellie would eventually appear in forty-eight movies, acting next to the likes of Greta Garbo, Joan Crawford, Chaplin and Clark Gable. Nellie Bly Baker became a household name in silent movies.

While filming on location in the Eastern Sierra in 1932, Nellie fell in love with the majestic scenery of the area. The following year, she and her husband, John Henderson O'Bryan, vacationed in Mammoth Lakes, hunting, fishing and, at least for Nellie, enjoying the beauty of the outdoors and the mountains. Soon, the call of the mountains reignited Nellie's love of adventure and her free spirit, and by 1935, Nellie had moved to the Eastern Sierra. There is no mention of John O'Bryan after Nellie moved, so it has been assumed that they divorced, either because of the move or shortly after their vacation, of which John had not been a fan. A few years after moving to Lundy Canyon, Nellie and John reconciled and spent the rest of their years together.

Nellie Baker purchased property near an old mining camp in Lundy Canyon, close to Mono Lake. Nellie wasn't quite sure what she wanted to do, but she did know that Hollywood no longer seemed to matter to her. Using skills she learned by building her own pool and guesthouse at her Hollywood home, Nellie began building her own house in Lundy Canyon. Her first winter in the Sierra was the coldest she ever spent in Lundy Canyon. No matter how many blankets she threw on her bed, it wasn't enough. Recalling her days in Hollywood, Nellie remembered that she had packed her full-length mink coat. Digging it out of her trunk, she turned it inside out and used the expensive coat as a bed shirt. Baker once quipped, "The first night I used that stupid mink, was the first time I had been warm in months."

Nellie didn't stop at building her house. Using the same wood from the abandoned miners' shacks she had used to build her cabin, Nellie erected an entire small camp, with cabins and a place for her guests to eat. Baker named her new lodge Happy Landing Resort. She cooked all three meals at the resort and served her guests and cleaned up. She also cleaned the cabins and the buildings to make sure her guests were as comfortable as possible. Nellie found that many of those coming to her lodge wanted to go hiking, fishing and hunting. Nellie began leading groups into the mountains and eventually became the first woman in the state of California to hold a license as a hunting and fishing guide.

Nellie built this cabin herself, and this shows how cold it can become in Lundy Canyon. *Courtesy of Mono Basin Historical Society.*

So dedicated was Nellie to making sure her guests were comfortable and had what they needed that her fame for hospitality grew beyond California. She managed to keep her resort operating through World War II. Her reputation was so impressive that people used their gas ration coupons to come for a weekend and sometimes longer. Many who came to the Happy Landing Resort and went off to war spoke of her place, so there were those who spent their leave time relaxing at her lodge. After the war, her fame continued. With the advent of the great American car culture, folks flocked to the Sierra, many coming to stay at Nellie's place. By 1952, Nellie was nearing her sixtieth birthday, and she was beginning to tire with the amount of work it took to keep the lodge running to her standards. She made the difficult decision to sell the Happy Landing Resort.

Nellie may have sold her lodge, but she didn't leave her beloved Eastern Sierra. She leased a lot on nearby Mono Lake and settled down for a long, relaxing retirement. Sedentary life did not suit Nellie Bly Baker, and once boredom set in, she began looking for ways to spend her time. Once, while guiding a group into the backcountry, she had seen a miner's cabin that had fallen from a high ledge and lay upside-down but intact. Thinking about the way the furniture had neatly arranged itself after the fall, Nellie began building a replica of this cabin in its upside-down configuration. She wasn't doing it for any other reason than for something to do that was artistic in nature. And, as Baker was wont to do, she dove into the project with gusto.

Once Nellie completed the structure, she brought in furnishings, fixtures, household goods and even a stove and painstakingly placed each item inside the topsy-turvy cabin until she was satisfied with her fantasy cabin. Her reputation being what it was, once Baker was finished, tourists from all over began coming to see her upside-down cabin. At one time, it was the number-one attraction in all of Mono County. Nellie, for her part, was always gracious in welcoming those who came to see her work.

Retirement never did suit Nellie, and she continued leading guided pack trips into the backcountry, fishing trips to the many lakes of the area and hunting treks during the season. When she wasn't leading expeditions, Baker was writing for the Bridgeport newspaper, helping set up the Mono County Chamber of Commerce and helping keep the wilderness from being overrun with careless visitors. Nellie's last guide job came at the age of seventy-one, when she led a group of ten hikers ten miles to over ten thousand feet. Nellie was a force of nature even then. She was eventually forced to retire when she suffered a stroke in 1982. She spent her last two years in a convalescent home in Lone Pine, California, passing away in 1984 at the age of ninety-one.

Nellie loved to paint, and "Indian Chief" can still be seen today with a trip up Lundy Canyon and a stop at the Beaver Dam.

Nellie saw this cabin while trekking through the backcountry of the Sierra. After she "retired," she built an exact replica from memory.

Nellie furnished the inside of her upside-down cabin as close to the original as she could. Nellie's unusual cabin can still be seen at the Mono Basin History Museum in the small town of Lee Vining, California.

Nellie Bly Baker may not have been as famous as the other Nellie Bly, but in all ways and more she was just as impressive. She was an independent woman at a time when that was frowned upon, but she never let that get her down. She became a movie star, carpenter, mason, camera operator, hotelier and outdoor mountain guide. She built a piece of art from a sighting in the wilderness that can still be seen today next to the Mono Basin Historical Museum in Lee Vining, along with a painted rock titled *Indian Chief* near the Lundy Canyon beaver ponds. She left a legacy in the area that is hard to miss. Nellie Bly Baker is in all ways a legend of the Sierra and of Highway 395, as much as any you will find.

7

WILLIAM HENRY "BURRO" SCHMIDT AND HIS TUNNEL

Some say that William Schmidt was crazy, others that he was a smart man protecting a valuable claim; whatever the case may be, "Burro," as he came to be known, certainly was obsessed with digging a hole. William Schmidt was born a few miles outside of Providence, Rhode Island. After his three brothers and sisters died of tuberculosis (known at the time as consumption), he moved out to the California desert in the hopes that the warm, dry climate would help prevent him from catching the disease. The disease is also the reason that Schmidt never married. He was afraid that he would pass it to his offspring, something he could never do to his children.

Schmidt arrived in Kern County in 1895 and took a job with the Kern County Land Management Company. He worked there for just two years before heading home, but he returned to California for good in 1900. Not wanting to go back to work for Kern County, Schmidt settled on some land above Last Chance Canyon in the El Paso Mountains and staked a mining claim called Copper Basin Claims. Schmidt built a small cabin next to the hillside, used old newspaper and magazine clippings for insulation and used a tiny stove to cook meals of mostly flapjacks and beans. To say Schmidt lived a frugal life is an understatement.

As Schmidt mined his claim, he bought two mules to help get his ore to the smelters. Schmidt was unhappy about the delay the long trip caused and began looking for another way to get his ore down to the rail tracks, where a train then transported it. To this end, Schmidt decided that a direct route

A MONUMENT TO
DETERMINATION AND PERSEVERANCE
WILLIAM HENRY "BURRO" SCHMIDT
IT TOOK THIRTY-EIGHT YEARS TO HAND DIG THIS
HALF-MILE LONG TUNNEL, COMPLETED IN 1938.
BORN IN RHODE ISLAND, JANUARY 30, 1871
DIED IN RIDGECREST, CALIF. JANUARY 27, 1954
AND SO RECORDED MAY 16, 1970
E CLAMPUS VITUS
PETER LEBECK CHAPTER 1866

This marker outside the entrance to the tunnel was erected by E Clampus Vitus in 1970 to honor and remember a man with an obsession.

through the mountain would be the best option. So, at the age of thirty-six, he began to dig near his cabin. Schmidt would dig, blast, dig some more and then sleep for the night. The whole process was repeated the next day and for the next thirty-two years of the man's life.

Schmidt became so obsessed with his "short cut," as he called it, that he completely ignored many rich veins of gold, silver, copper and iron, or so it is said. Schmidt would only stop digging when spring came to Kern County, and then he would grab his two burros, Jack and Jenny, head to the Kern River Valley and hire on as a ranch hand at whatever farm was hiring. When the fall season arrived, Schmidt would pack up his meager belongings, grab his pay and head to Teagle's store in the town of Johannesburg to buy the beans, coffee and flapjacks that would see him through the winter. He then would head back up to his cabin to continue the work on his tunnel. Schmidt was never seen off the mountain without his burros; they became part of the legend springing up around him. People began to call him "Burro" Schmidt.

Digging through solid stone is not an easy task, especially if one is taking on the work alone. Schmidt used a small jackhammer to drill two small, three-to-four-foot-deep holes in the tunnel face and then placed dynamite into the holes, along with blasting caps and fuse to pulverize the rock. Schmidt was very careful not to overdo the dynamite and used a 40 percent stick to get the work done. After the tunnel face was blasted, Schmidt hand-dug the rest and carried out the dirt by hand or with a wheelbarrow, but never with his burros. The animals were too important to Schmidt for him to use them in such grueling work. It is said that later in life, after so much physical labor, Schmidt's abdominal muscles became so strong that they caused him to have a permanent bend, resulting in great pain. Eventually, to make his job easier and to help alleviate the pain, Schmidt began installing rails and finally a small ore cart.

Schmidt became obsessed with his tunnel. No matter how many people said it would amount to nothing, he wouldn't stop. At some point, the man must have realized that the work far outweighed the benefit, but he didn't stop digging his shortcut to nowhere, as it was being called. The obsession overcame Schmidt. He began to bypass rich mineral veins that, if mined for their profit, would not only have allowed him to stop working farms and ranches in the summer months but also might have made him a wealthy man. It is for this reason that many believe that Schmidt was purposely lying about the creation of the tunnel as a way to deter claim jumpers, squatters and other miners from coming in and edging into his claim. The one problem with this theory, however, is that Burro Schmidt seemed to have died a very poor man. If he had indeed been mining his claim, where did his fortune go? Where was his money?

Schmidt never seemed to have enough money to keep a healthy supply of food, coffee or clothing on hand and couldn't afford the kerosene for lamps. To light his way in the pitch-black tunnel, Schmidt bought cheap candles—three for five cents—and made one last an entire day. Working almost entirely in the dark and using a leveling system of a bowl of water placed on the track he laid down, Schmidt completed the cart rails and finally the tunnel itself. For two thousand feet, the tunnel is dead straight then, just before the end, Schmidt put in a sharp turn. The exit comes out high above Koehn Dry Lake. The views of the lake and the town of Cantil, along with Randsburg and the Rand Mountains in the distance, are spectacular. On clear days, even Mount San Jacinto is visible. Even with the views, the exit, being so high above the valley floor and all but inaccessible for transporting ore or anything else, proves that for the thirty-two years Schmidt dug his short cut, it was indeed a fool's errand to create a short cut to nowhere.

After the tunnel was completed, Schmidt did begin mining his claim again. But he never did transport the ore through his tunnel. Later in life, Schmidt took on a partner, Mike Lee, to help with the operation. When Schmidt

This sparse, hand-built "cabin" was where William Schmidt lived until he died and was then home to Evelyn "Tonie" Seger until she passed.

The entrance to the tunnel is short; one needs to stoop to enter.

passed away in 1953, just a few days shy of his eighty-second birthday, he left the claim, the cabin and the tunnel to Lee. Shortly before his death, Schmidt offered his tunnel to the University of California mineralogy department to be used in its studies. The school turned it down, but the gesture showed his generous nature.

After Lee's death in 1963, Evelyn "Tonie" Seger and her husband, Milo, bought the Schmidt and Lee cabin from the probate court in Bakersfield sight unseen for $5,000 and moved up to Copper Mountain and the tunnel nearby. The Segers moved to California for the same reason as Schmidt had, namely, for Milo's health. With no water and few conveniences, the Segers were dependent on trucked-in water and a generator for electricity. Life was hard for the couple on the mountain, away from civilization. They hoped that the dry, warm climate would help with Milo's health problems, but it was not to be. One day in 1964, Tonie found her husband on the ground next to their old truck. As he lay dying in her arms, Milo told her that his one wish had been that they found water for their home. He asked Tonie to continue the search. Tonie did just that and became a legend in her own right in the area.

After Milo passed, Tonie became obsessed with his dying wish. Every day, she would give tours of the tunnel, then wander the area with her dowsing

The tunnel itself is not much taller than the entrance. If you venture in, it is recommended that you wear a hard hat.

rod looking for water. Day in and day out she searched until, one day, she found a well. Say what you will about dowsing, but it has worked on many occasions, this being one of them. When asked how she found the water, all Tonie would say is, "I witched it."

Over the years, Tonie, a retired navy nurse, tried her hand at mining but never failed to find time to speak with the tourists who flocked to the tunnel. Tonie began giving lectures about Burro Schmidt, his tunnel and the surrounding desert and became known as the "Tunnel Lady" by some and the "Old Lady on the Hill" by others. She even wrote a piece about Schmidt and the tunnel for a Time/Life book, *Odd and Eccentric People*.

Evelyn Seger was a feisty woman with a determined, independent streak. Longtime friend and confidant Davis Ayers once said, "She could be as nice as she wanted to be but she could be as nasty as she wanted to if that was called for." He also said that Seger was "one woman you don't want to get angry at you." This feisty attitude was a big help when, in the late 1970s, a woman with a nearby claim tried to run Seger out of the area. Tonie had potshots taken at her by members of the other woman's family and woke up one night with one of her buildings on fire. Other forms of vandalism were also committed around her property. It all came to a head one day when the would-be claim jumper showed up at Seger's door with a loaded gun.

The end of the tunnel comes out on a high embankment overlooking Highway 395. Schmidt's idea led him nowhere, as his shortcut was too steep to traverse.

As soon as Tonie saw the weapon, she knocked the pistol from the other woman's hand, leaned in and menacingly told her, "If you ever show up at my door with a gun again, you better be prepared to use it. Because I will." After this incident, things settled into an uneasy truce that lasted until Seger passed away in May 2003 at the ripe old age of ninety-five.

With the passing of Evelyn "Tonie" Seger, the land and the tunnel, as well as the tourists, were tended to by Dave Ayres. Unfortunately, the Bureau of Land Management (BLM), using what many call "shady" tactics, found a way to make Ayres leave the property. With no caretaker, the cabin and buildings erected after Schmidt passed away were vandalized and ransacked and were designated by the BLM as "nonhistoric" and, as they were now situated on public land, deemed "unsafe." Today, the historic Schmidt cabin that visitors could once explore is off-limits and fenced off. The tunnel that once wowed tourists is still open, but a four-wheel drive vehicle is needed to reach the location. Signs ask visitors to be respectful and not damage the tunnel or area. The BLM does patrol up to the tunnel on occasion, but the area is left open for those intrepid souls who make the journey. The tunnel and the views make the trip worthwhile.

8

SIERRA PHANTOM

There are many characters to be found along Highway 395. Some may be a bit strange, others, slightly amusing. And still others are hard to define but memorable nonetheless. But there is one character that I would place in all of these categories. Sierra Phantom is one of those people who are almost impossible to define. At times, he was aloof. At other times, he was so outgoing and talkative that one could get wrapped up in his stories and hope he never stopped talking. At other times, he could be moody and just as quickly become jovial. He was a man of many dimensions, a man more comfortable alone in the wilderness than among people, and yet he was so open and kind when in a crowd or with those he called friends. Sierra Phantom was a true enigma and can only be described as an introverted extrovert.

John P. Glover was born on July 20, 1926, in Orange, California, to German immigrants, Eric and Heidi Glover. John always said that he never knew what the "P." stood for; this was because he never really knew his parents. For the first three years of his life, John grew up in the loving presence of Eric and Heidi. They were constantly writing home to Germany about their son, the child's firsts, who he looked like and all the things parents tell their family. Unfortunately, the letters the Glovers received in return were not only unpleasant but also downright scary. They talked about the rise of Adolf Hitler and the atrocities that he, even at that time, was committing against anyone who opposed him. Because the Great Depression had hit

Germany so hard, Hitler was busy snatching up land and property and selling it to stash away to build his army for his later military conquests. Scared for their family in Germany, the Glovers decided to go back home and bring their family to America. To keep their son safe, Eric and Heidi left John in California with family friends who agreed to watch him for "a couple of weeks." The day after Eric and Heidi arrived in Germany, the family farm was raided by Nazi stormtroopers who killed everyone there, including John's parents. The Glovers' friends did not want or were not able to keep a three-year-old fed during the Depression, so John P. Glover was dropped off at the Department of Social Services and made a ward of the state. This would be the beginning of a long, hard road for the young John Glover and the genesis of the Sierra Phantom.

As a ward of the state, John was constantly being moved to different orphanages and foster homes. One of his earliest memories was when he was three or four years old, at the Waverly Baby Home in Los Angeles, California. He remembered escaping from his crib and being chased by nuns. He broke a bottle, which alerted them to his hiding place and also cut him enough to leave a permanent scar. As John put it, "It was my first attempt at escape." It certainly wouldn't be his last.

When John was five years old, he was transferred to Saint Agnes's orphanage, where he was constantly being picked on by the older kids. Knocking him down and making fun of him became a game to the older boys. It was here that John started to develop his determination and steadfast individuality to do things on his own, even with something as simple as learning to tie his own shoes or learning how to sew, in order to not give the bullies an excuse to make fun of him. Maybe it was the bullying or the prisonlike surroundings and atmosphere of the orphanages, but John began to have a deep need and thirst for freedom—to get away from everything and everybody. It became a challenge for him to find a way to get free of the state, to be on his own. Even at a young age, John yearned for the freedom to be himself. He swore that one day he would escape and be his own man. As John once said, "I have always had a real passion for nature. The thing that kept me going is the mystique of it. I grew up with a curious mind, wondering what's behind that next mountain, what's up there, what's down there? I have always been that way. I'm still that way today."

By the age of nine, John P. Glover had been transferred to the Luther Burbank School for Boys in Washington State. The school was along the shores of Lake Washington, and every May Day, the school held a field day. The orphans competed against one another for a trip into town for an ice cream, a movie or other fun things. Each win earned a series of points, and the student with the most points for the day was the winner. Glover really didn't care about winning a trip to town, but he figured that he would give one of the swimming events a go. John swam so fast in the fifty-meter freestyle event that he left everyone far behind, even those older than him. He had to wait for them to reach the dock and finish the race. Glover entered every other swimming event and took first place in each one. By the time he finished the last event, a news reporter was waiting for him. This was the first time John Glover saw his name in print, but it wasn't the last. John didn't care about winning or about a trip into town. It was about the freedom the swimming offered him. While in the water, he could forget about the school bullies, the sometimes cruel headmistress and the lousy food. In the water, all of John's senses were alive and free. In that moment, John felt the mountains calling him, felt the air on the peaks whispering his name and felt the cool alpine lakes flowing into him from where he had just been swimming. He vowed then and there to escape for good the life that fate had chosen for him.

It would take another six months of planning and waiting for the right opportunity for the nine-year-old Glover to make his break, but on a cold Friday movie night at the orphanage, the time had come. John snuck out of the orphanage and made his way down to the lake and the boats tied up at the dock. He quietly slipped into a small rowboat and plied the oars. At first, the going was fairly easy, but as he got farther out, the boat began to slow and the oars began to get harder and harder to move. Glover soon found out that ice on the bottom of the boat had been hiding a leak. The reason the boat was slowing and getting harder to row was that it was sinking. The boy was about equidistant from each shore and needed to make a decision on what to do—move forward or go back to where it was warm. Glover hated it at the school and so, without a second thought, jumped into the freezing lake and began swimming to the opposite shore from the orphanage. By the time he reached safety, he was freezing and close to hypothermia. He decided to find a place to rest and warm up. He would deal with where to go and what to do once he was rested.

The following morning, still cold from the night before and hungry from the exertion of rowing the sinking boat, Glover thought about what to do. He figured the first thing was to find warm clothes and some food, but with no money to his name, that might be difficult to accomplish. The boy thought that there was only one solution: take up robbing houses. It wasn't that John really wanted to do that, but he figured that, at his young age, no one would hire him, and he wasn't about to go back to an orphanage, nor was he willing to freeze or go hungry. In John Glover's young mind, there was simply no other choice.

Glover would approach a house he believed was a good target and knock on the door. If someone answered, he would simply ask for directions to his "friend's" house. When the homeowner said they didn't know the person, John would simply leave. If no one answered, he would try the door, which in that day in Seattle was usually unlocked, and enter the home, calling out to make sure no one answered. The first thing he would do was open a back door or back window in case he needed to make an escape and then look around for what he needed—food and clothing or things he found that would be useful. This went on for months, and Glover never got caught. During this time, the police were looking for him as a runaway. One day, while Glover was in a park beneath a tree he had been sleeping under, the cops spotted him. They weren't looking for him as a thief, but they did take him in and back into state custody. That pretty much ended the crime spree of John Glover. When asked about stealing by Danielle Nadler, author of *Without a Trace: The Life of Sierra Phantom*, Glover, in typical fashion, said it was just another learning experience:

> *You know, every person has a point in their life where they're learnin' the stuff that will become their livelihood, and most don't even know it at the time. Course I stopped stealing after a while, but I was sleepin' in the park, thinking ahead about how to get food and clothing, and really surviving on my own. Most kids would be afraid of all that, but I didn't know enough to be afraid. Think that's when I started learning everything I needed to know to make it in the High Sierra.*

After the police found young John Glover in the park, he was afraid they would take him back to Parkland School. The state had other ideas. Both relieved and leery about where they were taking him, John wound up somewhere that was worse than the school. The police dropped Glover off at a farm and foster care home run by an angry drunk and his overworked, neglectful wife, who saw the kids as nothing more than an extra paycheck. John didn't know at the time that this would be the beginning of a new, better life for him, one that would set him on a course with destiny.

It wasn't long until the Department of Social Services found out about these foster parents and removed all of the children from their care. When the car pulled up and took the children away, John was again afraid of where

After the Sierra Phantom was forced to leave his beloved mountains, he spent most of his time fishing the local lakes, hiking or hanging out at Schat's Bakery.

he would end up. After dropping off the younger kids, the social worker took Glover on a long drive, out into the country, finally bringing him to the Green Hills Detention Center. This was a facility for boys who had gotten into trouble by stealing, doing drugs or doing other things that got the notice of law enforcement. It was also a place where orphaned boys could learn new skills they would need for a productive life. The first thing Glover noticed was the lack of fencing; there was none in sight, nothing to keep the children from escaping. He thought about how easy it was going to be to leave this place behind.

Once inside the office, John met James Burton, the headmaster. The first thing Burton told John was, "Hey, if you wanna run, there's the door." It was the only school Glover never ran from, nor did he try. The school was there to teach, not to imprison. Burton's philosophy was to make sure that the boys learned as much about as many things as possible so that when they were ready to leave, they would have a choice of professions and be able to earn a living and make their way in life. John found a form of freedom in the school he hadn't known in any other. It was in the learning of new things and the fact that he was allowed to do it on his own, as he saw fit. The school was just what he needed.

While staying at Green Hills, Glover learned all sorts of new things. He was fifteen years old by the time he arrived at the detention center after a long, hard life of bullies and what amounted to a lifetime in prison conditions. Now, John was learning to milk cows, chop firewood, work in a metal shop, grow a garden and—what he seemed to take to the best—carpentry. Even though it was mostly hard work, John enjoyed working with his hands, learning new things and creating things. He even gained a friend. With Glover's help, the boy and Glover became the class comedians and performed not only for the school but also for local clubs, such as the Elks, Shriners and Masons. The "troupe" even managed to make a bit of money with their shows. Burton would also take the best-behaved boys on camping trips, where he would teach them survival skills, including one special trait that John Glover would carry into adulthood: the ability to leave no trace.

Glover's skill at carpentry eventually led him to be chosen for an apprenticeship with a shop owner, Claudley Hickman, in Seattle's Chinatown. Taking this job meant that Glover would no longer be a ward of the state but would finally be free. While John worked as an apprentice, he and Hickman became close. John learned to speak Chinese so that they could understand the purchase orders from the Chinese customers. All was humming along until December 7, 1941. As John listened to the radio one evening, he heard a recruitment ad that promised, "See the world, and protect our nation." John jumped at the chance to join. Hickman had to fib about John's age for him to enlist, since he was only sixteen. The minimum age to join was eighteen. Once enlisted in the U.S. Navy, Glover was a natural. Because he had volunteered, he was assigned as squad leader of his training unit and, due to his expert marksmanship, was made the sharpshooter of a ground unit.

When Glover was told his unit was being sent to Alaska to help defend and reclaim what the Japanese had taken, he was thrilled. He had always wanted to see that frontier and thought his time spent there, in the beautiful surroundings, would be a great adventure. That would turn out to be far from the truth. The war would haunt him for the rest of his life.

John Glover spent all four years of the war in Alaska, and after it was all over, he wanted nothing to do with society, governments or people in general. He wanted nothing more than to be by himself, surrounded by trees, peace and the beauty of nature. Glover was fed up with humanity. Once he was back in San Francisco, he got a job at a Walgreens so that he could build up a nest egg for the time he would begin living in the wilderness. He gathered dry supplies and boxed them up, each box holding $100 or more taped to the inside of the lid. He gathered approximately thirty-five of these boxes and gave them to a friend, who promised to hold on to them and send them to Glover when needed and asked for. When all was set and Glover had prepared himself for what awaited, he set off for the High Sierra.

THE SIERRA PHANTOM IS BORN

Over the next fifty years, John Glover lived mostly alone, other than for his trips to Bishop, Lone Pine or one of the other small towns along Highway 395 to gather supplies for the coming winter. He set up eight different camps in the Sierra stretching for what he said was just over one hundred miles. He fished, hunted, gathered berries and built shelters and igloos to live in. One of the reasons he set up so many camps was that rangers didn't allow camping for more than two weeks in one location. John, being always on the move, was never caught, yet all of the rangers knew he was there. Since he never liked his name and never knew what the "P." stood for, along with the untrue belief that his parents had abandoned him, Glover called himself Sierra Phantom. Publicly, he said that he gave himself the name because he was like a phantom that the rangers could never catch. The truth, however, is more mundane. It turns out that Glover always loved the comic strip hero Phantom. Whatever the case, from the day he set off into the wilderness of the High Sierra, John Glover was known as Sierra Phantom. Phantom to his friends.

Although Sierra Phantom shunned society, he didn't shun people. There were times while he was living in the wilderness that his help was needed, and he gladly lent a hand. When, in 1982, a sudden snowstorm came upon the Sierra, hundreds of tourists became lost, trapped and otherwise caught flatfooted and in danger. Phantom took it upon himself to go up and look for as many people as possible to rescue. As he explained, "So all these flatlanders were up there for a spring weekend…in flip-flops and T-shirts, completely unprepared. Well, this snowstorm comes, and all these people, hundreds of 'em, get stranded up there.…Because I know every nook and cranny of the High Sierra, I ended up hiking right to the worst of the storm to lead people out.…I saved almost seventy people by the end of it." Most times, things weren't that desperate, and Phantom, whenever he ran into others, would stop and give them advice about the mountains, tell them how to judge the weather or give advice about his favorite subject and pastime, fishing.

Sierra Phantom became an expert fisherman. It was more than a pastime; it became a passion. Phantom knew and fished every lake and stream the Sierra had to offer. He even knew those that no one else did, save for the Paiutes, who also called the mountains home. Phantom invented his own lures that, later in life, he sold in the town of Bishop. He was asked many times if living alone in the wilderness made him lonely. He often got mad at the question. But, as was his way, anger would give way to patient frustration, and he would simply answer, "Hell no, the mountains are my family, who'd get lonely with them around?" or some variation of that theme. Phantom was truly happy when alone in his High Sierra.

Unfortunately, as with everything in life, age creeps up on us all, and nothing we do or say can change that. So it was with the Sierra Phantom. Phantom moved to the High Sierra when he was twenty-one years old. Before he had a chance to develop the instincts and intuition the mountains would instill in him, the Sierra tried to kill him—or it may have been one of its first lessons. While fishing a stream near Mount Whitney, Phantom heard a low rumble. Looking up, he saw an avalanche heading his way and took off running. When his foot caught on a rock, he tumbled down a forty-foot ledge and watched as the giant wave of snow and stone washed over him. Figuring his time had come, he braced for the end that he thought was coming. When it was all over, he was still alive, but his pack and all of his belongings, including all of his money, were gone. The mountains had taken his gear but had spared his life. As Phantom sat there with a precipitous drop in front of him and an almost sheer incline behind him, he almost gave up. It took him almost a day of deciding not to give up, but finally, Phantom dug deep and climbed up the wall behind him to relative safety. With missing fingernails and bloody hands, Phantom made his way down to Lone Pine so that he could once again stock up and head back into the wilderness.

Fifty years later, with his instincts fine-tuned, he knew what was coming. He knew this would be his last day on earth. The storm hadn't caught him by surprise, but it had moved much quicker than expected. Phantom had been hurrying to get back to camp, but as the snowstorm grew, so did the drifts that slowed his progress. As he lost feeling in his hands and feet, he tried to press on but was so tired he figured a moment's rest couldn't hurt. As he lay there looking up at the sky through the mountain trees, he thought, "This is how I want to go, peaceful in my Sierra home." Phantom closed his eyes with no regret. What seemed to him as only a moment later, he heard a worried voice calling to him, "Sierra Phantom…Phantom?" It was his Paiute friend Sanuye. His friend urged him to get up, and although he didn't want to, Phantom knew that Sanuye wouldn't stop until he did. Together, they began walking down the mountain. This was the last thing Sierra Phantom remembered before he woke up in the hospital in Bishop.

That was the last day that Phantom lived in his beloved Sierra. The doctors told him that, at his age, he wouldn't even make it another month if he tried to go back and live alone in the wilderness. So that was that, as they say. Phantom stayed in Bishop. But not really having the means or the ability to get housing, he slept in the parks and hung out at nearby Schat's Bakery. Phantom began to tie the fishing flies he had developed over the years and sold them to tourists and "flatlander" fishermen while sitting in front of Schat's. This brought in a bit of needed cash. But even though Phantom had tried to stay as far away from the government as possible, he knew he needed help. Trying to get Social Security was not easy. Since he had grown up as an orphan and a runaway, it was hard to prove he was who he said he was. Even his military record wasn't enough for the government. Finally, a gruff agent at the Social Security office was able to get him a small monthly stipend, and she also arranged for a small apartment in a "senior" complex. Phantom, for the first time in his life and in old age, was living in society as norms dictated. He hated it…at least at first.

Phantom spent most days riding his old Huffy bicycle up to one of his favorite fishing spots, South Lake being his go-to. He tied his "Glitter Flies," as he called them, and sold them outside the bakery. Phantom would talk to anyone who would listen about his life up in the wilds, the proper way to fish and why his flies were the best at catching all the fish they could carry. Some people thought his stories were no more than tall tales, and perhaps a lot were, but Phantom didn't care. He knew who he was and enjoyed the telling. He became a regular in Bishop, and most in town knew him or knew of him, and everyone he met in Bishop liked him. It may have been fate, but a serious hit-and-run that caused Phantom to need major eye surgery may have brought him to the person who was undoubtedly his soulmate.

After Phantom partially recovered from the hit-and-run, he still needed surgery to repair his eye. The trouble was that he needed to find a ride to Los Angeles. One day, while talking to the owner of the bakery about how he was going to get to the hospital, a woman rolled up in an old Ford truck and offered to drive him. She explained that she lived in the trailer park behind the bakery and had nothing else to do and would be happy to

Phantom sold his "guaranteed" fishing lures at these tables outside of Schat's Bakery.

lend a hand. As they drove from Bishop to Los Angeles, Phantom and the woman, named Reynier, or Rennie for short, became fast friends. Phantom and Rennie would spend the rest of Phantom's life fishing, hiking, eating dinner at Denny's (Phantom's favorite eatery) or just hanging out. It was obvious how they felt, but it wasn't until the day before Phantom died that they finally said "I love you" to each other.

As the days passed into years, Phantom became almost a legend in the town of Bishop. He led hikes and tours up into the mountains, took fishermen up to "secret" lakes, escorted Boy Scouts and helped them earn wilderness badges, sold his flies, told his tales and fed anyone in town who he thought needed food. He fed them fish, of course. The servers at Denny's became like family to him, and he would drop off his catch to those with large families to feed and delivered fish to the doors of those he met around town who needed a hand. Rennie once quipped that he was the "Robin Hood of Bishop." No one would go hungry while the Sierra Phantom could fish.

Maybe it was his lifetime spent in the wilderness or his many years of smoking "healthy Paiute" cigarettes, not to mention twice being struck in hit-and-runs—Phantom contracted pneumonia and was hospitalized. During his stay, it was found that he also had lung cancer. Phantom had been talking with Danielle Nadler, who had agreed to write his story. Being the type of person he was, the night before he passed, Phantom apologized to her for not being able to talk. He died the morning of January 30, 2012. That day, the world lost not only a true legend of the High Sierra but also a man who grew up rough and in pain, only to come out the other side kind and gentle, caring about others. The man was a true survivor.

The Sierra Phantom was cremated, and a group of his friends—and he had many—took him to his favorite fishing spot on South Lake. There, they gave him the best gift they could, and one Phantom would appreciate the most: an eternity fishing in his beloved High Sierra.

PART II

ROAD TRIPPING HIGHWAY 395

9

LONE PINE AND
THE ALABAMA HILLS

Lone Pine is a small town on the northern end of Owens Lake. It was founded in the 1860s as a supply point for the mining towns of Cerro Gordo, Darwin and what is now the ghost town of Kearsarge. Named for the single pine tree that stood at the mouth of Lone Pine Canyon, the town now serves as the portal to the highest peak in the contiguous United States, Mount Whitney, as well as a camping and fishing hub for those heading to sites in the Alabama Hills or the Eastern Sierra. The town itself is small, but it has a rich history, from the nearby Manzanar Relocation Camp to the silver mining ghost towns of Cerro Gordo and Keeler, to the Movie Road area where hundreds of television and feature films were made. Lone Pine is truly a gem within the harsh landscape of the Owens Valley.

Set at the foot of the Eastern Sierra, below the majestic Mount Whitney peak, the Alabama Hills is a wonderland of adventure, serenity and history. Camping, rock climbing, hiking and exploring some of your favorite movie locations, from those for *Star Trek* to a Wild West shootout from your most-watched Western, can be found among the hills. Perhaps one of the oddest attractions in this area is what has come to be known as Nightmare Rock.

Nestled in the hills is a rock that resembles a squat, fat head that local artists have decided should have a face placed on its front side. The face is both rudimentary in its artwork and classic in its urban appeal.

The giant painted creature has a smile that invites the onlooker to grin while at the same time shiver at its razor-sharp teeth. The grin will

Nightmare Rock has become a local legend along Highway 395 and a canvas for Lone Pine artists.

immediately return as you glance up and spot the KISS makeup around the left eye and the long, protruding tongue that seems to mock your amused fright.

Urban art is one of those things that teeters between graffiti and expressionism, provoking anger at the defacing of nature and pleasure in the simple beauty of the artist's work. Nightmare Rock is no exception. So, go out to the Alabama Hills and climb this rock, sit atop its massive face and remember, it's meant to bring a smile to your face and place a memory in your mind. Although the rock's face may change from time to time, the spirit of its creation remains.

Since the first silent film was shot in the area, a western titled *The Roundup* starring Fatty Arbuckle, the Alabama Hills has been portrayed as the American Wild West, the Himalayas, Arabia, India and Africa. It has even depicted multiple alien and nightmarish landscapes of worlds beyond imagination.

Because of the area's jutting stone teeth rising like spires out of the ground and its many arches and strange landscapes, the hills have been used in science fiction movies such as *Star Trek V* and *VII* and *Star Trek: Generations*, *Tremors* and the Superman movie *Man of Steel*. It is featured in the blockbuster film *Gladiator*, all three of the *Lone Ranger* films beginning in 1938, along with *Iron Man* and *Django Unchained*. It has been featured in more Western movies than can be listed here.

Feature films aren't the only entertainment filmed along Movie Road. Many television shows have called the Alabama Hills home as well. Classic shows that owe their atmosphere to the rugged landscape include *Wagon Train*, *Alias Smith and Jones*, *The Lone Ranger*, *Rawhide* and *Bonanza*. Many more films and television shows have used the unusual topography of the hills to add color, flavor and mystery to the stories being told.

The number of famous stars who have tread the soil here is almost beyond belief. John Wayne, Roy Rogers, Gene Autry and Tom Mix had shootouts and fistfights in the dirt here. William Shatner, Patrick Stewart and Leonard Nimoy fought alien creatures and renegade scientists among the strange formations of rocks in this area, and the likes of Gregory Peck, Anne Baxter, Humphrey Bogart and Ida Lupino fell in love surrounded by the beautiful Sierra Mountains. It would be hard to believe that anyone reading this book has not seen this amazing panorama on film at least once.

As you turn off of Whitney Portal Road and merge onto Movie Road, there is now a memorial marker that dedicates this site. The plaque was

In the early days of moviemaking in the Alabama Hills, modified cars and trucks were used to film in the rough terrain. This RKO camera wagon is a good example of early Hollywood ingenuity.

With the Alabama Hills' eerie, otherworldly appearance, it was the perfect location for the strange "Graboids" used in the movie *Tremors*. At the Museum of Western Film History, one can look at the Graboid used in the film, along with many iconic movie and TV props and paraphernalia.

dedicated by Roy Rogers, who had his first starring role here in 1938. There is also a 10,500-square-foot museum along Highway 395 as you enter Lone Pine from the south. The Museum of Western Film History has displays and movie posters from the very early days of filming in the area up to today; props and uniforms from *Star Trek*, *Star Wars* and *Tremors*; a 1928 Lincoln camera car; Panavision and Technicolor cameras; along with early twentieth-century projectors. You will find guns and rifles used in the movies, a stage coach and even a mockup of the creature from *Tremors*.

If you decide to visit, try to plan your trip for the Columbus Day weekend. If so, you will have the added pleasure of being able to attend the annual Lone Pine Film Festival. This is one of the most important Western film festivals in the country and one of the most fun. So, if Hollywood films and memorabilia are your thing, you will find the museum and Movie Road right up your alley.

Lone Pine is a must-see for anyone driving through the Owens Valley on their way to Reno, Lake Tahoe or Virginia City. I would also highly recommend Lone Pine as a weekend getaway. The town has much to offer: scenic vistas with unrivaled beauty; history of not only California and Hollywood but also of national interest; and some of the best camping and fishing the state has to offer. There are also some great eateries and hotels. If you visit, I promise you won't regret it.

10

SILVER, CHARCOAL AND A THIRST FOR WATER

CERRO GORDO

About twenty-five miles southeast of Lone Pine sits the old mining town of Cerro Gordo. Known as one of the "Big 5" must-see ghost towns in the United States for enthusiasts, this remote silver/lead mining town is a time capsule of not only the Owens Valley but also of California itself. Discovered by Pablo Flores in 1865, Cerro Gordo, meaning "Fat Hill," became the largest producer of silver in California and the largest producer of zinc carbonate in the entire United States.

At its peak, the town's population reached 4,500 people, with a mix of nationalities, including Hispanic, Anglo, Indian and Chinese workers living in bunkhouses and shacks. The small town grew to have several general stores, saloons, restaurants and two hotels. One of these, the American Hotel, upscale lodging designed for the well-to-do and built in 1871, still stood at the now defunct mining camp. Unfortunately, the hotel burned down in 2020. But it is being rebuilt. The camp also sported a doctor's office, lawyer and assay offices, two dancehall/brothels and a blacksmith shop. The town oddly had no church, school or jail.

Today, Cerro Gordo is a shell of what it once was. The town is open for guided and self-guided tours and includes the old general store filling in as a museum, the original assay office and hoist house, along with the abovementioned American Hotel. The American Hotel is reportedly

Left: The town of Cerro Gordo would become the largest sliver-producing mine in California history. *Courtesy of Eastern California Museum.*

Right: This photo shows the spectacular views from the town of Cerro Gordo and the once vibrant and full Owens Lake before the City of Los Angeles stole the valley's water. *Courtesy of Eastern California Museum.*

haunted, as are a couple other buildings. So if you have that as an interest, Cerro Gordo delivers. The views of the Owens Valley below the town, Mount Whitney and the Sierra Nevada Range are spectacular. If you go, don't forget your camera.

Although the town is open year-round, it is always a good idea to check on road conditions and weather. It does snow up on the mountain. It is a short eight miles up the "Yellow Grade Road," named for the yellow shale in the area. The road is now simply called the Cerro Gordo Road. It can be a bit treacherous. Four-wheel drive vehicles are recommended, though not required, as the county-maintained dirt road gains a mile in altitude and has many narrow cliffside areas that can get steep, as well as ruts, potholes and rocks that can be present in the trail. For those interested in going up to this historic ghost town, the road starts just a mile or so outside of the historic, barely living ghost town of Keeler.

KEELER

Keeler is not your typical ghost town. It is what some people call a "living ghost town" because there are still people who live there. I personally like to say it is a "barely living ghost town." I say this because, as the older generation still living within the town limits pass away, so will the town.

Keeler began life as Cerro Gordo Landing. Because the town was along the shore of Owens Lake, a dock was built, and the town became the main loading dock for shipping ore across the water to Cartago. Cerro Gordo Landing eventually changed its name to Keeler in honor of Captain Julius Keeler. In 1883, a rail line was extended to Keeler, and the town became the last stop for the Carson & Colorado Railroad. For all intents and purposes, the town of Keeler looked to have a bright future. Unfortunately, that was not meant to be.

When the silver coming from Cerro Gordo played out, the town began to decline. Even after the largest zinc deposit in the United States was discovered in the area, it lasted only until the 1930s. To make matters worse, the booming city of Los Angeles, just over two hundred miles away, had begun stealing the water from the Owens Valley to satisfy its thirsty citizens.

For a time, and partly because of the water theft project going on, a large number of workers and tourists began flocking to the area. The leaders of Keeler used this influx of people to turn their little town on the lake into a resort. The Hotel Keeler provided lodging for those arriving by both car and train, the Keeler Community Pool became a popular attraction and, with Owens Lake bordering the town, this became the main attraction for Keeler. Again, this period of prosperity was not to last long.

When the Los Angeles Aqueduct was completed, most of those working on the project left and never returned. Some came back for recreation, and tourists were still coming to the area. But as the water was being diverted to the big city, the Owens Valley began to dry up. The lake drastically receded from the town until Keeler lay well over a mile away across salty, alkali ground from the now muddy pool that the lake had become. People no longer wanted to come to the town. Dust storms began to sweep through the area, and it became so bad that many residents left the town and still others began to suffer from respiratory illness caused by the corrosive dust. Many people developed cancer and passed away. The town was literally dying, all because of the selfishness of the big city. Keeler is now classified as the dustiest place in North America, second in the world only to the Bodélé Depression in Chad.

The last train pulled out of the Keeler depot in 1960, the hotel burned down and the pool was drained. Keeler today is nothing more than a few homes, most abandoned, some crumbling walls and an old, run-down train station. A plaque was erected in 1973 for the *Slim Princess* (the name of the locomotive that ran to town) by a chapter of E Clampus Vitus, and a now faded surfboard was placed by a local near the pool that sadly but amusingly

Left: The community pool in the town of Keeler, once a popular tourist stop, has become an algae-filled weed pond. With the City of Los Angles's theft of the valley's water, the town of Keeler is slowly dying.

Below: The Keeler Train Depot was the terminus for the Carson & Colorado Railroad in Keeler's heyday.

Opposite: These massive "beehive" kilns were used to create charcoal that was then transported across Owens Lake to Keeler and from there to the mines at Cerro Gordo.

read, "Keeler Beach—Swim, Surf, Fish-Camps for rent. A victim of Los Angeles' thirst for water." The last gas station in town closed down, removing the last reason for anyone to stop in Keeler.

Keeler thrived while the silver, zinc and water were still present in the Owens Valley. When greed and avarice prevailed, the valley suffered, and the once thriving town began to die. Even though this small town may pass into history, Keeler's legend will remain as a lesson against greed and selfishness for those who would heed the lesson.

Cottonwood Charcoal Kilns

Resembling giant hornet's nests looming out of the desert landscape just south of Lone Pine along what once was the western shore of Owens Lake are two large adobe kilns. These ovens were built in 1873 by Colonel Sherman Stevens. Stevens also built a flume along Cottonwood Creek to help get his logs from the mountain hillsides, so it was not a reach for him to use these same logs to produce charcoal—hence, the charcoal ovens.

The kilns fired the lumber into fine-grade charcoal, which, along with lumber for mine shoring, was then shipped by the steamers *Bessie Brady*

and *Mollie Stevens* from Stevens Wharf, across Owens Lake to Keeler. The charcoal was then transported up to the Cerro Gordo mines and used in the mills. The wood that was needed for this process was fed into the kilns through a hole in the top of the ovens. This gave the kilns easy loading and venting to help regulate the temperature of the ovens. Doors in the front of the kilns allowed the charcoal to be removed.

These kilns are now some of the only remnants of what was, in essence, the old mining organism that was the lifeblood of the valley, each piece fitting together to create a whole. Unfortunately, the kilns were abandoned over a century ago, and time has not been kind. Decay, neglect and the harsh climate of the area have caused the sides of these beehive structures to collapse. It is not clear how much longer they can remain standing, but efforts are in place to help preserve them. Still, it is worth the one-mile side trip to visit these legends of the Owens Valley, if for no other reason than to get an idea of the size of these massive kilns.

11

THE TOWN OF INDEPENDENCE

The town of Independence started as a small trading post in 1861 and went by the name of Putnam's, in honor of the trading post's founder, Charles Putnam. It wasn't long until the name was changed to Little Pine for the creek the town was established near. Five years after the original settlement was created, the town name was changed once again, this time to the one we know today, Independence. The name comes from the army fort built nearby, established on July 4, 1862.

Independence, even though it is a very small town with an even smaller population, became the county seat in the late 1800s when its chief rival, the town of Kearsarge, was buried under an avalanche. The town still holds that designation and has one of the nation's most picturesque and postcard-worthy examples of an American Colonial–style courthouse. Small the town may be, but there is more to Independence than meets the eye.

Fort Independence

Three miles north of the town of Independence, California, lies what remains of the original Fort Independence. Established on July 4, 1862, along Oak Creek during what became known as the Owens Valley Paiute War, the fort was used for only a short time before it was abandoned.

All that is left of Camp Independence is this marker and a few of the caves that troopers were forced to live in.

The fort, manned while the structures were built, forced the troops to use caves and dugouts along the creek as makeshift lodgings. Some of these crude living quarters are still there for visitors to see today. After the barracks were completed, the army began diverting water, growing crops and establishing outposts in the area. All of this drew the attention of the Paiute population, and they began flocking to the area for the available food and water supplies.

In 1863, one of the most tragic events in colonial and Native American relations took place when Captain Moses McLaughlin ordered the Paiute people to march from Fort Independence, through the treacherous landscape of eastern California, to Fort Tejon two hundred miles away. McLaughlin was a man despised by not only the Paiute but also his own men. He was an admitted Indian hater and treated them with contempt and malice. Of the 1,000 Paiutes who began the journey, only 850 arrived at Fort Tejon. Of the 150 who were lost along the way, some managed to escape, yet most perished. The trek became known as California's Trail of Tears.

As a result of the hatred among the men toward their often drunk captain, and the removal of the Native Americans from the Owens Valley,

Troopers of Camp Independence were forced to use these caves as makeshift barracks in the early days of the fort.

Above: Now mostly destroyed by the ravages of time, these caves were the troopers' homes before barracks were constructed. One can only imagine how the troopers felt when they finally had proper housing at Camp Independence.

Left: Early travelers along the El Camino Sierra stop to rest at the crumbling walls of Camp Independence. *Courtesy of Eastern California Museum.*

Fort Independence was shut down in 1864. It would not remain shuttered for long, however. As the Paiutes began leaving Fort Tejon to return to their ancestral home, the fort was reopened in March 1865. Used primarily as a West Coast garrison for protection in the Civil War, by 1877, Fort Independence had outlived its usefulness and was abandoned for good.

What is left of the fort is part of the Fort Independence Indian Reservation. The land was officially turned over to the Native Americans in 1915–16. Today, the reservation has created a wonderful casino/resort, Winnedumah Winns Casino, for weary travelers and has one of the largest travel plazas in the country, selling everything from fuel and sundries to fast food and upscale grilled food.

The first building erected at Camp Independence was the administration building. The troopers would have to stay in their caves a bit longer. *Courtesy of Eastern California Museum.*

Fort Independence is almost completely lost to history. A remnant was moved from the camp and now sits in the town of Independence, at 303 Edwards Street. This Commanding Officers Building can still be viewed and provides a good sense of what it must have been like in those times and lets visitors know just how serious the town takes its history.

THE WINNEDUMAH MONUMENT

Lore from the Owens Valley Paiute tribe says that long ago there were two tribes that lived in the area. One tribe, the Paiutes, in what is today the Owens Valley, and the other tribe, the Waucoba, resided on the western side of the mountains. These two tribes were at war, and each would set up lookouts to alert their tribe of a pending attack.

One day, a Waucoba brave spotted two Paiute brothers ascending the crest of what is now called Mount Williamson. The Waucoba strung his powerful bow, nocked an arrow made from a tree that only grows on the

Top: One can see how the legend of Winnedumah came to be after looking at this early photograph. *Courtesy of Eastern California Museum.*

Bottom: The Winnedumah Monument has become as much of a legend for travelers along Highway 395 as it is for the Paiute people. This photo shows early travelers posing in front of the monument after a grueling climb. *Courtesy of Eastern California Museum.*

west side of the mountain range and released it. The arrow winged its way to the target, fifteen miles away, and struck one of the brothers, killing him instantly. The Paiute fell face-down on the ground with his head to the east and his feet pointing west, and he was turned to stone.

The other man, seeing his brother felled by the arrow, became terrified and tried to run. The Waucoba, seeing the man flee, yelled out in a booming voice of thunder, "Winnedumah!" In their language, this meant, "Stay right where you are." Hearing the Waucoba demand, the Paiute was instantly turned into a pillar of granite and still stands, next to the body of his brother, awaiting his release by the Great Spirit. The arrow that struck the man's brother, imbedded in the stone body of the fallen Paiute, over time became a tree and still stands as the only tree of its kind in the Inyo Range.

This tale is an important part of the lore told among the Paiute people even today. The Winnedumah Paiute Monument, where this story had its genesis, is only about twelve miles east of the town of Independence. To get there, one follows Mazourka Road up to a parking and camping area and then makes a roughly eight-mile round-trip hike to the monument. If you aren't able to make the hike, or just want to take a peek at this eighty-foot monolith, you can get a good view of it from the intersection of Highway 395 and Mazourka Canyon Road. Please be careful of traffic if doing so.

Whether you hike or get a quick view from the road, you will be rewarded by the sight of this truly epic rock.

Mary Austin

Born in 1868 in Illinois, Mary Austin (née Hunter) and her family moved to California in 1888, soon after Mary graduated college. Austin became a prolific novelist and playwright as well as a naturalist, an early feminist and a champion of Native American rights. Mary and her husband, Stafford Austin, became intimately involved in the Owens Valley water war with the City of Los Angeles. The disappointment and loss of the battle eventually destroyed her marriage, with her husband moving from their Owens Valley home to Death Valley and Mary settling in Carmel, California.

Austin wrote extensively about Native American life, in novel form, such as *The Land of Little Rain* (1903), and in short story collections, and she wrote books featuring regional sketches, such as *The Flock* (1906). Other works by Austin include the romantic novel *Isidro* (1905) and the collection *The Basket Woman* (1904).

After her separation from Stafford, Austin traveled to Europe, where she met H.G. Wells and others who helped strengthen her beliefs in both socialism and mysticism. On her return from Europe, Austin lived for a time in New York City. New York helped to further solidify her views. After moving back to Carmel, Austin helped found the historic Forest Theater and was part of a group of authors and artists, including Jack London, James Hopper, Alice McGowan and Sinclair Lewis. Austin is said to have been involved in what became known as Carmel's "Bohemian Society," which included unencumbered sexual liaisons and "homoerotic" friendships.

Though Austin's views may have been a bit out of the mainstream of the country, her time spent in Europe and New York was the catalyst for some of her best work. Her play *The Arrow Maker* (1911), and what many consider to be her best novel, *A Woman of Genius* (1912), seem obvious products of her time spent among the socialist elite of those two places. After scores of didactic articles written by Austin, as well as her novels *The Ford* (1927) and *No. 26 Jayne Street* (1920), it is obvious where Austin leaned both politically and socially.

Austin finally settled in Santa Fe, New Mexico, in 1924, where she wrote several more tomes having to do with Native American culture and her social beliefs. Austin even penned an autobiography, *Earth Horizon* (1932). Many of her works dealing with Native Americans have been compared to those of Ralph Waldo Emerson and John Muir. Austin's dedication to preserving Native arts, crafts and culture would have made both men proud.

Left: Mary Austin has become a legend in the town of Independence, California, as well as in the Owens Valley. *Courtesy of Eastern California Museum.*

Right: Mary Austin was an early proponent of the women's movement. This was not a popular idea in her time, and she was dubbed a "bohemian." *Courtesy of Eastern California Museum.*

Mary Austin passed away in 1934, but her legacy, so important to those who remember her, is still alive and thriving in the Owens Valley. Austin's house is still present at 253 Market Street in Independence and was granted State Historic Landmark Status 229. The home stands only eight and a half miles from Mount Mary Austin in the Sierra Nevada, which was named in her honor.

PUTNAM'S CABIN

Charles Putnam was the first to settle in what eventually became the town of Independence. Putnam's stone cabin was the first permanent structure built in Inyo County and was used from 1861 as a home, hospital, trading post and "fort for early settlers coming to the area." The cabin became the center of the town of Putnam's. This name lasted only five years before being changed to Independence. The structure was torn down in 1876. All that remains today is a monument, designated California Historic Marker 223, located at 139 Edwards Street (Highway 395), which is directly across the street from the Inyo County courthouse.

CARSON & COLORADO RAILWAY

This narrow-gauge railroad was begun as a way to connect the Carson and Colorado Rivers. The owners laid out the route so that the line would cross what they hoped would become some of the best mining country in the world, the Owens Valley.

Incorporated in 1880, the Carson & Colorado began in Mound House, Nevada (near Carson City), and its terminus eventually became the small town of Keeler, on the shores of Owens Lake. This arid, three-hundred-mile route was dependent mainly on minerals for its economic life, but a growing farming community helped bolster the outlook for the area. The first train arrived at Keeler in August 1883 and greatly aided in the transport of the massive amount of silver coming from the nearby Cerro Gordo mines. Along the route, the C&C Railway made several stops in Nevada and in Owensville (Laws), Kearsarge, Manzanar, Dolomite and Swansea, California. The route reached an altitude of 7,100 feet at the Montgomery Pass.

The railway never turned much of a profit, and the original owners hung on for twenty years before they lost interest and sold out to the Southern Pacific Railroad in 1900. Unfortunately for them, just after the sale of the C&C Railway, a large ore strike took place in Tonopah and Goldfield, Nevada, allowing the Southern Pacific to expand the line, recoup its investment and change the narrow-gauge line to a standard, broad gauge between Mound House and Mina, Nevada. The span from Mina to Keeler remained a narrow gauge and was merged into the Southern Pacific subsidiary, the Nevada and California Railroad. Then, in 1912, it was reorganized as the Central Pacific Railroad, and the line operated under the name Southern Pacific, Keeler Branch.

The Southern Pacific Railroad kept the narrow-gauge line running unchanged until the Great Depression hit. With the economy tanking, the profits began to dwindle, and between 1938 and 1943, the Southern Pacific was forced to shut down the northern end of the route. This reduced the

Old No. 9 is an original steam locomotive of the Carson & Colorado Railroad that ran from Mound House, Nevada, down to the now dying town of Keeler, California.

route to a mere seventy miles between the town of Laws, just outside of Bishop, and Keeler.

The narrow-gauge line continued to run for a dozen more years, but with the coming of the automobile, mining in the area dwindling dramatically and the trucking industry dawning, the last narrow-gauge locomotive made its final run on April 30, 1960. By the end of 1961, most of the tracks had been removed, and the remnants of the once touted Carson & Colorado Railway all but disappeared.

Today, one can still see some of the history surrounding this once important part of Owens Valley. Through the efforts of rail enthusiasts and preservationists in the towns of Laws and Independence, you can still see some of the artifacts from the Carson & Colorado. One of the stars of the old railroad sits in the town of Independence at the Eastern California Museum. Here, you will find the new home of the Carson & Colorado Railway. The preservationists are so dedicated to bringing back the history that they have fully restored the Southern Pacific narrow-gauge locomotive number 18. It is one of only a handful of these locomotives to be fully operational. This locomotive, rare as it is, was loaned out to the Silverton & Durango Railroad, which used it on its daily tour runs as a way of showcasing the history of narrow-gauge travel in the United States. Old number 18 now sits outside the museum in a place of honor for all to see.

The original operator of the Carson & Colorado, Virginia and Truckee Railroad, has been reformed and now runs a tourist service in the style of the old C&C line from Virginia City, Nevada, to the station in Mound House. So, if you want to get a feel for what it must have been like "back in the day," this is a good way to do just that.

12

MANZANAR RELOCATION CAMP

World War II was a time of great conflict and pain brought on by evil, prejudice and hate. Unfortunately, many people never realize that the United States, in its fear and hatred of those who killed so many with the Japanese surprise attack on Pearl Harbor, allowed its own prejudice to come to the fore. The hatred toward the Japanese Empire for thrusting America into World War II reached not only the Japanese Islands and its holdings but also those loyal Japanese Americans living in the United States, a country to which they were fiercely loyal, the only country many had ever known, a country they called home.

When the Japanese Empire attacked the Hawaiian Islands, it sent a shockwave around the world, but not as strong as the wave that hit the United States. Not only shock, but also anger and uncontrollable rage shot through America. When people are afraid, they do things that might otherwise not be in their nature—things they are ashamed of after the dust has settled and reason has returned. Only then do they realize that those they wronged were not only innocent men, women and children but also patriots ready to die for the country that has wronged them. This is the legacy of Manzanar Concentration Camp, colloquially called a "relocation camp."

As a result of what many called a barbaric, unprovoked and sneak attack by the Japanese, and fueled by both farming and fishing conglomerates upset about Japanese Americans' success in those endeavors lobbying Washington to do something about the "Japanese problem," President Franklin Roosevelt signed Executive Order 9066 on February 19, 1942. The order authorized

When Executive Order 9066 was signed by Franklin Delano Roosevelt, Manzanar was euphemistically called a "relocation camp." In actuality, it was a concentration camp for American citizens of Japanese descent.

the secretary of war to "exclude any and all persons" from designated military areas and to set up the War Relocation Authority to construct relocation centers to house those excluded. The order resulted in the forced relocation of more than 120,000 Japanese living in the United States, most of whom were American citizens. Many of those displaced from California were sent to the remote camp in the middle of the Owens Valley near the old town of Manzanar.

This area of the Owens Valley along California Highway 395 is no stranger to people who have been forced to leave their homes by the federal government. In the 1860s, after gold was discovered, miners, farmers and cattlemen began to flock to the area. The influx of settlers began to encroach into the lands of the Paiutes, and they began to fight back against what they saw as invaders. After the conflict was won by the U.S. Army, the Paiutes were force-marched out of the area (by way of the longest possible route) and sent to Fort Tejon.

Manzanar (Spanish for "apple orchard") officially became a town in 1910, when agricultural developer George Chaffey founded it five years after purchasing Shepherd's Ranch and many of the surrounding ranches. Within a year, the small town had just less than two hundred residents. A post office, a telephone line, a "one and a half story" public building, a barbershop and a lodge were built, and more people arrived to set down roots. By 1920, Manzanar had more than twenty-five houses, a schoolroom, a town hall, a general store and five thousand acres of rich farmland. As former resident Martha Mills said, "Manzanar was a happy place to live during those years, with its peach, pear, and apple orchards…tree lined country lanes, meadows and corn fields."

The happy times did not last long, however.

Los Angeles was essentially built on desert terrain and, as such, lacked sufficient water for the growth the city saw in the early 1900s. The city, looking for ways to bring more of the life-giving liquid to its population, set its sights on the Owens Valley. Los Angeles had secretly begun acquiring water rights throughout the valley, and by 1920, farm after farm in the valley floor had been bought up by the metropolis, stretching all the way into Mono County. By 1933, Los Angeles owned most of the ranches and many town properties in the Owens Valley. One of these towns was Manzanar. As Los Angeles began to pump the valley dry, independent farmers were left with crops they couldn't water and, with the giant city pumping out the groundwater, no hope for ever growing enough to make a living. By 1929, Manzanar had been abandoned and would stay that way until 1942, when the City of Los Angles leased the area to the U.S. government.

After Order 9066 was enacted, the War Department was frantic to come up with a solution for housing the thousands of Japanese it was rounding up. Temporary housing at Santa Anita and Tanforan horse-racing tracks had been set up as "assembly centers," but these were woefully inadequate for long-term housing. To solve this, the War Department began buying and leasing land wherever it could find it. One of the areas it leased from the City of Los Angeles was the town of Manzanar.

Manzanar Relocation Camp was opened on March 21, 1942, after a frenzied and rushed construction. Markedly better than the horse stalls and pens the Japanese had to endure at the assembly areas, the community barracks were still barely fit for the families that would take up residence here. Poorly insulated, cramped and sparsely furnished, these facilities looked and felt just like the POW camps captured combatants were housed in. The medical facilities weren't any better. Dr. Yoshi Togaski arrived early to prepare for the arrivals but found that the supplies were completely inadequate for the number of people expected to be housed at the camp. Necessary medications and vaccines were donated and sent to

The U.S. government told Japanese Americans that the camp was for their protection. If this had been true, guard towers with guns directed *into* the camp would not have been necessary.

camp by friends willing to help. Within three weeks of internees arriving at Manzanar, the makeshift hospital had treated children for chicken pox, measles, whooping cough and other ailments. As time went on in the camp, a proper hospital and medical staff were slowly assembled. This was of great comfort to those who had only known America's first-rate healthcare system before being interred.

As time went on, Manzanar settled into as normal a routine as possible for those living in what was essentially a concentration camp. A camp government was established by which some of the everyday decisions regarding living conditions were decided. A newspaper was established. In addition, public gardens were created and a beautification committee was tasked with making the camp a more pleasant place to live. Life became as pleasant as they could make it, considering the circumstances they found themselves in. Unfortunately, there were conflicts within the camp, as only American citizens could be in the camp government. In addition, U.S. policy did not allow Issei (a Japanese immigrant to America) or Kibei (Japanese born in America but educated in Japan) to hold formal leadership positions. These policies created a lot of resentment within those classes of people. The Issei and Kibei began to accuse those in the JACL (Japanese American Citizens League) of being informants for the WRA (War Relocation Authority) and the FBI. It came to a head on December 5, 1942, when JACL leader Fred Tayama returned from a meeting in Salt Lake City and was attacked and beaten by Harry Ueno and two other men. Ueno was arrested and sent to jail in the town of Independence; the two others were questioned but released overnight. Later that day, a large crowd gathered, then worked itself up and grew larger. Then things got out of hand. By 9:30 p.m., tear gas was fired into the crowd, spurring the mob to send unmanned cars toward the camp police station. The cars were fired upon by MPs. Hearing gunshots, two other MPs took it upon themselves to open fire into the crowd. As the throng dispersed, eleven people were shot, two fatally.

The director of the WRA had the notion that the occupants of the camp needed "loyalty training." This idea points out the complete misunderstanding that the WRA, and the rest of the country, had regarding the extent to which the Japanese Americans who were locked up truly loved their country. This loyalty question would forever be answered by the formation of the segregated, Japanese-only 442nd Regimental Combat Team (RCT).

The 442nd RCT was formed in 1943 as a result of mounting losses in the Pacific and European theaters of war. The Japanese American 100th Battalion, formed in Hawaii, was combined with volunteers from the

Barracks such as this one were spread out all through Manzanar. These barracks housed up to three families each, with little more than curtains separating them for privacy.

Trying to make Manzanar feel as much like home as possible, the internees created flower and rock gardens, along with decorative pools and fish ponds, like the Arai fish pond seen here.

Although most of those buried at the Japanese cemetery at Manzanar have been reinterred elsewhere, a few loyal patriots remain buried here with the beautiful Sierra Mountains as a backdrop.

relocation camps within the United States, many from Manzanar, to form the 442nd RCT. This regiment, known as "Go for Broke," originally hoped to be sent to the Pacific theater to fight against the Japanese Empire in order to get revenge for the attack on their home, the United States. This was not to be. The 442nd was sent to the 5th Army to fight in the rough terrain of the Italian campaign. Once there, the members of Go for Broke fought so valiantly for their country that they became the most decorated unit in American history for their size. The 442nd became so famous for its bravery, determination and loyalty that its legend lives on to this day.

Manzanar continued to sequester loyal Japanese Americans in the sometimes harsh Owens Valley climate until the Supreme Court, in *Endo vs. the United States*, ruled that the WRA had no right to detain citizens who were deemed to be loyal to the United States of America. The ruling was handed down on December 18, 1944. Manzanar opened its doors and allowed all of the internees to return to the West Coast as soon as they were able to relocate. Manzanar was finally closed for good on November 21, 1945.

Today, Manzanar is kept as a National Historic Site administered by the National Park Service. Not much is left of the original camp, but among the facilities to see are a mockup of the barracks, the rock garden created by the internees, the guard house at the entrance with a guard tower and a gymnasium that has been turned into a museum. A must-see on the self-driving tour of the grounds is the Japanese Cemetery at the back of the camp. A few souls are buried here from the time Manzanar was in operation. The monument erected for the fallen is a grim reminder of what can happen, even in a society that values freedom above all else, when people allow their fear to govern their reason.

13

TUTTLE CREEK ASHRAM

This amazing building sits at an altitude of almost eight thousand feet above the vast stretches of the Owens Valley. Reached by a rugged trail just outside of Lone Pine, the Tuttle Creek Ashram is a monument to not only one couple's idea of peace but also true human determination. It is not an easy hike, but those who make the trek are rewarded with an amazing sight amid the beauty and splendor of the Sierra Forest under majestic Mount Whitney.

The ashram had its beginnings in 1929, when Franklin Merrell-Wolff and his wife, Sarah (Sherifa), arrived in Lone Pine. The Wolffs had a deep love for nature and spiritualism and found that the Sierra and surrounding Panamint Mountain ranges gave them a sense of peace and serenity they could not find elsewhere. Because of this, the couple packed supplies, a tent and a typewriter onto a burro and headed out to Hunter Flat (now Whitney Portal), at the base of Mount Whitney. They set up camp along Lone Pine Creek near a waterfall and settled in for a two-month retreat. There, Franklin began his first book, *Re-embodiment*, and he and Sarah began contemplating life, peace and other human emotions while working on their various writing pursuits.

Surrounded by the animals, birds and beauty of the Sierra, the Wolffs decided to establish an educational foundation to teach others their philosophy of peace and harmony. They called the organization the Assembly of Man. They also wanted to establish a place to bring their students closer to nature, a summer school, as it were. They knew it had to be here, at the highest point in the contiguous United States. The Wolffs had been told by an old Native American shaman that the spiritual center of any country was at its highest point of elevation, and it was here, at Mount Whitney, where they would build their school.

Franklin began making inquiries into what it would take to set up a camp in the wilderness where they had stayed but were told by the National Forestry Service that for a long-term camp like the one they wanted, a permanent building would have to be erected. Unfortunately, no permits could be issued for Hunter Flat, where they had camped for two months, so Wolff began exploring other areas nearby. When Franklin came to Tuttle Creek, he knew he had found what he had been looking for. Here, surrounded by a beautiful piñon pine forest, with two crystal-clear creeks, was an area where they could build their house of worship in quiet and solitude. The forest service granted the Wolffs permits to build and operate their summer school in Tuttle Creek in 1930. It was another ten years before the area was leveled enough to start building, even with the help the Wolffs were getting from friends and volunteers eager to build the ashram.

Franklin handled all of the dynamite chores himself. He would blast out an area, pile the stone, level and move on to the next spot. As the pile of stones, rocks and debris began to amass, Franklin had an idea. Since all of the debris came from the mountain and was part of it, why not use it in the construction of the building? When the foundation was finally ready, the four main pillars were laid out in the four cardinal directions, and the building was laid out in the shape of a balanced cross. The entire structure was built with spiritual meaning in mind. Wolff wanted every aspect of the school to impart a sense of serenity and peace, and that included how the school was constructed.

Even though rocks and stones from the mountain were used to build the school, it still required a large amount of cement and wood for proper construction. In the beginning, these materials were brought in on the backs of burros from nearby Olivas Ranch. This conveyance was slow and time-consuming. To help remedy this, Wolff began to clear away and widen a footpath to the south and eventually made it wide enough for a tractor pulling a flatbed trailer to operate on. This dramatically shortened the time needed to get the building supplies up to the structure.

The first major project was the large altar. This was built directly onto the floor of the structure using randomly patterned granite and held together by mortar. The walls of the ashram were built around this altar. The entire structure was two thousand square feet—not a simple task while hauling

The end of a short but steep two-and-a-half-mile hike brings you to the steps leading to the ashram.

supplies to an almost eight-thousand-foot elevation, out in the primitive area of the wild Sierra Mountains.

It would take twenty years for the ashram to be built. This had a lot to do with the fact that the project could not be undertaken year-round. The Wolffs and a group of volunteers would arrive in the spring, as early as the melting snow would allow. The entire construction process would have to be shut down by the time of the first snowfall. And it took time to cover and protect the areas susceptible to the severe winter weather of the Sierra and, most important, allow enough time for people to come down off the mountain. This meant that, at the very least, there was a week or more when construction could not occur while winterizing the site.

As hard as the physical labor could be, there was always a sense of belonging and joy in the camp while construction was ongoing. That is not to say that disputes did not arise or that human squabbles didn't happen, but the meaning of the project, along with the philosophical teachings of the Wolffs, seemed to bring all of those working a calmness within themselves that became the norm rather than the exception. Franklin and his students, as they had come to be called, would spend their days in hard work building the school and spend their evenings enjoying one another's company around the dinner table, playing music around a campfire and studying under the tutelage of the Wolffs.

At the end of each work season, the group would hold the Convention of Man. This was an annual celebration of Light and Dharma held over the last nights before everyone headed home for the winter. The group encouraged those from Lone Pine and the surrounding area to attend the celebration, and many of the local townsfolk came up and enjoyed the festivities and the company. In 1940, a student chronicled in film an entire summer of work on the ashram. The student documented not just the construction, but also daily life at the site, along with one of the formal weekly services. During that year, the entire group had to evacuate the area due to a forest fire. Once the fire was extinguished, they went right back to work. This is another reason the ashram took so long to construct. Anyone interested can see the film at www.merrell-wolff.org/ashrama.

As the work continued over the years, the ashram finally took shape. A twin-beam, gabled roof was put above stonework walls, a large stone fireplace was built and, just south of the altar, a thirty-two-inch square hole was installed. This hole was called the "cornerstone." The cornerstone is where those addressing the congregation stood while delivering their message. The window and door casings were complete and set to have the glass and doors installed when, in 1951, all work abruptly stopped on the ashram.

The health of Franklin's wife, Sherifa, had been failing since the late 1940s and took a sharp downturn in 1950. By 1951, Sherifa could no longer make the journey up to the ashram. Wolff credited Sherifa with being the drive and inspiration behind the project. He was more of an introvert, and even though he traveled the country lecturing when he was not at the ashram site, it was Sherifa with her overt personality who drew the acolytes, and Franklin, to Tuttle Creek year after year. With his wife unable to make the trek, Franklin stopped construction, and the site was all but abandoned. The Wolffs confined the work of the Assembly to their San Fernando Valley home. When, in 1956, Sherifa asked to live near the sea, the couple moved to Santa Barbara. It was there, in 1959, that Sherifa passed away and the dream of the Sierra ashram with her.

When all work stopped on the ashram in 1951, many people began to wonder what would become of the structure. When Congress passed the Wilderness Act in 1964 and Tuttle Creek became part of the John Muir Wilderness, the ashram was threatened with demolition. As buildings are not normally permitted in wilderness areas and the school had not been used in over ten years, the U.S. Forest Service invoked a clause allowing it to

Left: The fireplace and gabled roof, pictured here, were the first features of the ashram to be constructed.

Below: The altar and "cornerstone" were the heart of the ashram.

terminate Wolff's special use permit. The ashram was then scheduled to be demolished using dynamite. During an increasingly rare visit to the location by Wolff, he made a plea to save the site, and with a strong outpouring of support for the ashram by Lone Pine residents, the forest service decided to leave the building intact.

Over the years, from 1951 on, friends, family and visitors hiked up to the ashram and cleared away debris and trash left by careless hunters and campers. Sometime in the 1960s, a visitor to the ashram chiseled an inscription into the altar: "Father, into thy eternal wisdom, all creative love, and infinite power I direct my thoughts, give my devotion and manifest my energy that I may know, love and serve thee." To this day, it is not known who laid the inscription on the altar.

Sometime in early 1970, a Los Angeles film crew came to the ashram to make a short documentary about Tuttle Creek in the hopes of helping to preserve the site. Then, in the early 1980s, the U.S. Forest Service reevaluated the ashram for historical significance and concluded that the structure was indeed a site worth preserving for future generations. To this end, the forest service sent a request to the state capital in Sacramento detailing the history and historical importance of the ashram. The California State Historic Preservation officer concurred, but as of this writing, the site has still not been added to the registry.

Over the intervening years that the ashram has been waiting to officially claim historic status, several documentary films have been made to help preserve the site. *The Philosopher's Stone* (1980) and *Ashrama Man* (1983) can be viewed on the Franklin Merrell-Wolff Fellowship website. Unfortunately, many more are no longer available. In 1998, an article in the *Inyo Register* claimed that the ashram was still in danger of demolition. This brought an immediate response from the U.S. Forest Service: "The Forestry Service would be looking at preserving this…unique architectural property." The forest service planned to nominate the Tuttle Creek Ashram for placement in the National Register of Historic Places. Unfortunately, these plans have also not yet come to fruition.

The building has had many names over the years. It was originally called the Ajna Ashrama. As it was being built, Wolff's followers simply called it the Ashrama. Lone Pine residents sometimes refer to the structure as the Stone House or the Monastery, and the forest service refers to it as the Tuttle Creek Ashram.

Of those who brave the hike up to the ashram today, many say they can feel the spirituality that those who built the school must have imparted into

The front of the ashram, seen here, overlooks the vast expanse of the Owens Valley.

the very stones of the structure. They feel there is a presence of peacefulness and serenity. This must be why the spot was chosen to begin with. This sense of calm may be why quite a few locals still hike up to the ashram on a regular basis. As you cross the stream and catch your first glimpse of the ashram, you can sense the great feeling of accomplishment that must have existed after the erection of this truly historic structure. Let us hope that the wait for official designation by both the State of California and the federal government doesn't take much longer. It would be an absolute shame to lose this dream of the Wolffs and their followers to something as mundane as red tape.

14

TOM'S PLACE

Some things just go together, like a hand in a glove or peanut butter and jelly. The same goes for the Sierra Mountains and Tom's Place. This small stop along Highway 395 just twenty-three miles south of the Mammoth Mountain Ski Resort has become a traditional breakfast stop for visitors before they hit the slopes for a wet, snow-filled weekend of fun. For others, it is a prime location to stay while hunting in the area or fishing the clear blue lakes and streams. And good luck trying to book a room at Tom's Place on Fishmas weekend (the opening of fishing season). Few who pass by, stop for a meal or stay at the lodge know just how historic Tom's Place is.

Shortly after the highway was completed up past the Sherwin Grade, traffic began to pick up along the Eastern Sierra. As the traffic grew, so too did the need for goods and services along the highway. In 1917, German immigrant Hans Lof, traveling the road, came to the top of the grade, took one look around and decided that this would be a perfect place to build a fuel station and a rest stop for weary travelers. He soon found that his idea was a good one. With so many travelers making the stop at his new station, he added a cookhouse and, shortly after, a store. Many of these travelers were coming up to hunt and fish, so Lof built a corral, bought some horses and pack animals and began offering guided trips into the surrounding mountains. Hans Lof operated the small rest stop and fuel station for only six years and then sold the place. I cannot find a reason why he sold the successful venue, but in 1923, Thomas Jefferson Yerby and his wife, Hazel, whose Hollywood stage name was Jane Grey, purchased the property from Lof for $5,000. Not content to run a gas station and cookhouse, in 1924, Tom and Hazel built a lodge where guests could stay and renamed the new resort Tom's Place.

When the fish hatchery in the town of Independence opened and the lakes and streams began to be stocked for sport fishing, nearby Rock Creek became a prime spot for local anglers, fishermen from Los Angeles and visitors traveling to the newly completed Tioga Pass on their way to see the wonders of Yosemite. Tom's Place was booming with traffic and guests. Land just a few miles west of Tom's Place was developed into an auto camp named French Camp. With campers, fishermen, hunters and travelers flocking to the area, the store and café at Tom's Place was kept busy from spring through summer and well into the fall. With business being so good, the Yerbys added tent structures and permanent cabins to the resort.

Even with the Great Depression in full swing, Tom's Place managed to weather the storm. In the 1930s, two new resorts were being built in the area: Rock Creek Lodge and, a little farther up, Rock Creek Lakes Resort. Down at Crowley Lake, construction was continuing on the Crowley Lake Dam, and farther to the north, the Mono Craters Tunnel helped bring business,

After the fire of 1947, Ted Berner rebuilt the lodge. It is still the same cozy inn you can book to this day.

construction workers and guests to Tom's Place. When Prohibition ended in 1933, Tom and Hazel wrestled with the idea of opening a saloon for the resort. Hazel was not a fan of the idea, but the couple came to a compromise. Tom built the saloon across the highway from the resort proper. Tom Yerby passed away in 1940, but Hazel kept the business through World War II, with servicemen passing through on leave or heading to one of the many camps Highway 395 serviced. By 1945, the highway had been completely paved, car culture was in its infancy but growing rapidly and Tom's Place was already a well-known stop for travelers along the El Camino Sierra. Hazel had always done the cooking for the resort, and as she was getting up in years, and without Tom to help, she finally decided to sell the resort. Hazel put the resort on the market, and Ted Berner and his family bought Tom's Place for $80,000.

Berner ran Tom's Place with the same quality and care that the Yerbys had maintained, and business flourished until 1947. That year, while food was cooking at the resort, a fire broke out in the kitchen, and the old lodge burned to the ground. The cabins, saloon and other buildings were spared, but the damage was severe. Ted Berner wasted no time rebuilding what had become an Eastern Sierra landmark. When the new lodge was completed, Berner moved the saloon into the main building, the café was expanded and Tom's Place was up and running once more as the place to stop along the El Camino Highway. Ted Berner and his family owned and operated Tom's Place until 1985, when they decided to sell the historic resort.

An investment group operating under the name Tomco Inc. purchased the property, which it operated as a business, not as a year-round, hunting, fishing, camping and ski resort. Tomco decided to concentrate almost exclusively on the summer trade. It did offer limited services in the winter, fall and early spring seasons, but this was far from the services offered under the Yerbys and Berners. Tom's Place began a slow but steady decline under the corporate business plan, and although it was still a traditional stop for many in the know along Highway 395, it was not what investors had expected. The resort was put up for sale in 2000. Mark and Michelle Layne purchased the legendary property. They, along with their son Charlie, worked hard at renovating and refurbishing the resort and bringing it back to the prominent status it deserves. The Laynes have continued to uphold the legacy and historical integrity of this fixture in the Sierra.

Today, Tom's Place is again a central point for the local community. The location hosts and sponsors fundraisers such as barbecues, car shows, holiday parties and other events. The lodge that Berner built after

Above: Tom's Place café is still a popular stop for hungry travelers along California's Highway 395.

Left: Tom's Place has been designated a California historic site.

the 1947 fire is the one we see today, and many of the original cabins and buildings are still in use. Tom's Place is still a meeting place for those heading to the slopes at Mammoth Mountain. It is also a stop for carpool groups and families who have a tradition of coming in for breakfast—or any meal for that matter—while on a camping trip or a vacation in Virginia City or Reno, Nevada. For over one hundred years, Tom's Place has been welcoming weary wanderers with warm hospitality, a friendly smile, a hot meal and a warm bed.

15

CONVICT LAKE

L ake Wit-sa-nap, says a Paiute legend, is the home of Pot-sa-wa-gees, or water babies. These spirits are said to have the face of a Paiute child and the body of a fish. The spirits were peaceful and never bothered the Paiutes but were highly sought after by Hi-na-nu, a good and wise man whose spirit the Paiutes revered and someone they looked to for guidance in all earthly matters. Hi-na-nu was determined to possess a Pot-sa-wa-gee at any cost and traveled upstream as they fled, trying to capture them. As the water babies neared the stream's source, the water became so shallow that the spirits were afraid they would be taken by their pursuer. The Pot-sa-wa-gee prayed to the Great Spirit for help, and in answer, the shallows began to fill until a wide, deep lake was created. Thus, the Pot-sa-wa-gee were forever saved from Hi-na-nu, and Lake Wit-sa-nap was born. When Europeans arrived, they changed the name of Lake Wit-sa-nap to Mount Diablo, and the stream where the water babies fled became known as Diablo Creek. All that would change in 1871, after a mass escape from a Nevada prison sent shockwaves through eastern California.

On September 17, 1871, twenty-nine inmates escaped from the Nevada State Prison in Carson City. The prison, a maximum-security facility, housed the worst of the worst criminals. The escapees included horse thieves, train robbers, cattle rustlers and murderers. They killed and wounded several guards, then fled south into California. One of the leaders, convicted murderer Charlie Jones, had lived in Mono and Inyo Counties and knew the area well, so he figured they could hole up in the nearby mountains. They could collect enough food and supplies to make the trek over the Sierra and head into central California, where they could disappear. Back in Carson City, a posse was formed, but by the time it set out in pursuit, the trail had gone cold. The posse gave up the search after only a few days. It seemed that the runaways from justice might just stay free.

A couple of days after the posse had given up, the convicts were holed up along Diablo Creek, a short distance from the lake. One of the outlaws spotted a man on horseback heading their way, and the men set up to ambush the lone rider. The man on horseback was Billy Poor, a young mail rider who was delivering for the first and last time. The convicts, figuring that the rider, if allowed to continue, would give away their location, killed young Billy, took his clothes, dressed him in prison garb and left his body behind as they made their way to the lake.

When news of Poor's murder reached Sheriff George Hightower, Mono County formed its own posse, with Hightower heading it. The band consisted of merchants and locals along with a Native American deputy, Mono Jim. The lawmen headed into the mountains north of Bishop to search the vicinity where Poor's body had been found. As they searched, they found clues that the band of outlaws was still in the area. They finally caught up with them near the mouth of Diablo Creek. As soon as the convicts saw the posse, a shootout erupted between the groups, and bullets began to fly willy-nilly, neither group concentrating on accuracy but instead on firepower. The hail of lead lasted for a few minutes; when it was over, merchant and Wells Fargo agent Robert Morrison, along with deputy Mono Jim, lay dead. The convicts escaped.

Charlie Jones and his partner had avoided the gun battle, as they made their way down to Bishop earlier that morning, supposedly looking for supplies. In reality, they were trying to ditch the other convicts. Jones and his accomplice were eventually captured and executed for their brutal treatment of the prison guards and the murder of Billy Poor. The escapees involved in the shootout were arrested a short time after the ambush at Diablo Creek, and by November 1, eighteen of the twenty-nine escapees had been caught. Some were sent back to prison in Carson City; others faced execution for their part in the mayhem they created. And some, including those involved in the killings of Morrison and Mono Jim, were lynched on the way back to Nevada. As a result of the ambush and deaths of two well-respected members of the Mono County community, the tallest peak in the area was renamed Mount Morrison in honor of Robert Morrison; the smaller peak

The beauty of Convict Lake belies the tragedies that have occurred over the years at this once sacred site.

just below is now called Mono Jim Peak. The lake and creek were renamed Convict Lake and Convict Creek, respectively.

The prison in Carson City the convicts escaped from has a long and storied past. The Nevada State Prison was in operation from 1862 until September 2011 and is the only prison to ever have a casino installed for inmates. It shouldn't be surprising that Nevada, the first state to legalize gambling and whose economy is dependent on gaming, would allow inmates to gamble while incarcerated, at least for a time.

In 1932, the year after Nevada legalized gaming, the state prison in Carson City set up a casino to help rehabilitate prisoners by teaching them how to be dealers and gaming employees. The casino, called the "Bullpen," offered blackjack, poker, sports betting and even craps. Prison officials figured the inmates were going to gamble anyway, so why not keep an eye on them and teach them a trade at the same time. Many local citizens from various clubs like the Kiwanis, along with state officials and employees, came to try their luck at the Bullpen. Things went along well through the years, with very little cheating or unsavory behavior. Unfortunately, in 1967, the Nevada Prison Commission hired a new warden, Carl Hocker, formerly warden of California's San Quentin Prison. Hocker, not one to understand Nevada gaming or allowing inmates to gamble, immediately closed the Bullpen, sold off all of the gaming equipment and put an end to prison gambling. The sanctioned gaming of the Nevada State Prison came to an end, but the legend of the Bullpen remains, as does the Convict Lake ambush.

It would seem that Convict Lake has had its share of tragedy over the years of its existence, and what we hope will be the last took place in the winter of 1990. Camp O'Neal, a privately owned camp for troubled youth situated along the shore of Convict Lake, had a long history of abuse, neglect and sexual impropriety by its owner, Bobbi Trott Christiansen, and other "counselors." On February 19, 1990, three teens from the school, Shawn Diaz (fifteen), David Sellers (fifteen) and Ryan McCandless (thirteen), ventured onto the thin ice of the lake and fell through to their deaths in the frigid water. Counselors Randy Porter and David Myers, who may not have been watching the boys as they should have, also died in a rescue attempt. One of the counselors had a felony conviction and was found to have marijuana in his system during the autopsy.

Clay Cutter, an Inyo County Forest firefighter, was by his cabin chopping wood when one of the boys from the school ran up asking for help. Cutter immediately responded. Going out on the lake to try to rescue the boys and

If escaped convicts murdering those trying to apprehend them wasn't bad enough, the tragic and preventable loss of children and their would-be rescuers will forever scar this beautiful area.

counselors from the freezing water, he, too, was dragged under and died. Long Valley volunteer firefighter Vidar Anderson, who lived in a cabin at the lake, heard the commotion, went out to lend a hand and also fell through the thin ice and drowned. It took just over a week to recover all of the bodies from the lakebed. In all, three teenage boys, two counselors and two Inyo firefighters died that day. It may have been a tragic accident, but it was one that never should have happened.

Shortly after this incident, the State of California suspended the camp's license, alleging overmedication of patients, inadequate supervision and sexual misconduct by the camp psychiatrist, who was eventually arrested, convicted and imprisoned.

Today, Convict Lake is a beautiful, peaceful fishing lake in the majestic Sierra Mountains, with a resort of lovely cabins along the lake for rent and a general store with a "storybook" section with history about the lake and the many motion pictures it has been featured in. From the lore of the Native Americans, to the legends that surround the lake, to the wonderful history and great fishing, Convict Lake should be on everyone's list of places to see when traveling along Highway 395.

16

THE LOST CEMENT MINE

Mammoth Canyon in the High Sierra is dominated by the 11,034-foot, gray Mammoth Mountain. Geysers, pumice and sometimes boiling, steaming water shoot 80 feet into the air, sending minerals and other earthly sediments into the soil and ledges that surround these majestic mountains and hillsides. Mammoth is now known for its ski slopes and winter sports, hiking, fishing and other outdoor activities. But once, Mammoth was known for one of the richest gold strikes in history, albeit one that was never found.

In the mid-1800s, Mark Twain, in his book *Roughing It*, told a tale of three German brothers who split off from a wagon train heading west looking for a shortcut and adventure. They found what some say was the greatest gold vein in history. It is said that while taking a rest near a small stream, the brothers found a ledge "as wide as a curbstone" made of a rusty, reddish cement that was two-thirds pure gold. Knowing they didn't have the means, claim or time to harvest all the gold in the vein, the brothers took out approximately twenty-five pounds each, covered up the ledge and continued on. Two of the three brothers died before making it to the other side of the Sierra, but the third managed to stumble into a west-side mining camp, physically and mentally unstable from his ordeal. Even though he had lost much of the ore he had collected, what remained generated quite a bit of excitement among the miners in the camp. The brother wouldn't tell anyone where the rich ledge was, nor would he return to it, but he supposedly did give a description and a crude map of the location and area. Once word got out about the fabulous "Red Cement Mine," the rush was on to find it.

In 1879, the *San Francisco Post* published a piece by correspondent J.W.A. Wright, who was in Mammoth and who gave the following version of events:

The find was made by two men who had been with a California-bound train which came across the southern deserts. They left the train and reached the Sierra at the head of the Owens River. The year stated as 1857. In traveling through what they described as "the burnt country," they sat down to rest near a spring or stream. Here they observed a curious-looking rock and began pounding it up. They saw in it a quantity of what appeared to be gold. One insisted that it was gold; the other laughed at him. The believer took about ten pounds of the stuff with him. They crossed the rough mountains successfully and followed the San Joaquin River down until it brought them to Millerton. The one with the gold became consumptive and went to San Francisco for treatment. He hoped to return to the treasure, but became so ill that he had to give up the idea. Having no money with which to pay the physician who had taken care of him, a Dr. Randall, he gave him what ore he had left, a map of the country, and a description minute in particulars.

Dr. Randall arrived at old Monoville in spring of 1861. He engaged men to accompany him to what was called Pumice Flat, now said to be eight miles north of Mammoth Canyon. He located a quarter-section of land there, near what became known as Whiteman's Camp.

Randall came back the next year, and employed Gid Whiteman as fellow prospector and foreman and a force of eleven men. From that time, Whiteman became the foremost figure in the search that was still maintained when Wright's letter was written in 1879. With his map as a guide he and his men prospected the entire 160 acres. They found reddish lava or cement. Specimens shown by Randall were undoubtedly rich in gold; many reliable people who saw them declared them at least half composed of flakes of the precious metal. It is now supposed, said Wright, that these were pieces of the ore that the dying man had given him; but, as the man had told nothing, the impression was that he had found it in his late prospecting.

A tremendous excitement was the result. Prospectors poured out of Aurora and Monoville day and night. Never was there a greater furor about a mining find. During the whole summer of 1862 hundreds of prospectors hunted for the red cement; but they found nothing like it. From 1862 to 1879 not a year passed but from one to twenty parties spent part of the summer searching for the treasure. Some of the men abused the doctor and

Somewhere out here in the vast idyllic landscape of the Sierra Mountains outside the Crestview Rest Area just off Highway 395 lies perhaps the richest vein of gold ore ever discovered.

said that he was a humbug; others thought he was an earnest believer in the existence of such a ledge. Wright says of the Twain account: "The real facts of the original find were not so well known then as now. Friend Mark was giving us humor rather than history."

There is evidence that the Lost Cement Mine, as it was now called, was actually found in 1862 by two of the men hired by Dr. Randall and then hidden from him and all the others in their group. In authenticated statements, it is said that they secured thousands of dollars' worth of ore for themselves and that all that prevented them from acquiring more was their deaths at the start of the Owens Valley Indian War. Once again, the Lost Cement Mine was lost. Wright goes on to explain that at least seven men were killed by Indians while looking for the lost mine, although many other reports state that some of these men were murdered by other prospectors looking for the mine. Men will do evil things in the search for wealth, so it may be that many were killed looking for the riches of the Lost Cement Mine. One such nefarious character may be a man by the name of Farnsworth.

Farnsworth had been looking for the lost mine for quite a while when he met a man by the name of Robert Hume in Carson City, Nevada. Farnsworth found out that Hume had some money and showed the man rich quartz from a Mariposa County mine. Farnsworth said that if Hume put up the money for a small mill and would accompany him to help work the mine, he could have half interest. Hume accepted and gave Farnsworth $700 toward buying the mill. Not long after Farnsworth was given the money, Hume was found murdered. Farnsworth was the primary suspect. Farnsworth, of course, disappeared with the money not long after. In a letter to the editors, Wright relates this story:

Late in May 1869 two men giving their names as Kent and McDougall arrived in Stockton, California. They remained only long enough to outfit with horses, wagons, and provisions. They went to where the San Joaquin River leaves the foothills, arranged to leave their wagon and horses at a supply station there, and engaged a guide and pack stock. They told the station keeper they had friends in Mono and Inyo whom they wished to visit. The guide, an Indian, returned later with the pack animals and said he had taken the men to the pumice mountain [now Mammoth Peak]. Their visit was repeated every year through the summer of 1877.

Late in 1877, a man fell senseless and paralyzed on a San Francisco street. Prior to his ensuing death, he told a father confessor that he was McDougall and that he had become acquainted with Kent, who said he knew of a good thing in California. Kent wanted to go to the place, and engaged McDougall to accompany him on a guarantee of $1,500-a-year payment. McDougall related that when the guide had taken them to the vicinity of the pumice mountain they went a short distance north and established a camp on the San Joaquin side of the mountains. Kent said they were not far from what he believed to be one of the richest gold deposits in the state. He had found it in 1861, but the Indian war and other things had prevented him from reaping benefit from his knowledge.

The two began to build a rough cabin in a secluded spot, north of the old Indian trail that crossed the pass. To reach it they followed along the base of the range. Going up a small stream they crossed a second creek just below where it rushed down the mountain in a cascade. It fell over a peculiar little grotto in reddish lava. This grotto was a symmetrical concave, oval in shape, about five feet high, four feet wide, and three feet deep. A thin clear sheet of water poured in front. A small amount of fertile soil had accumulated at the bottom, and in it grew tufts of grass and other plants.

Their cabin was at length erected about twenty rods from this fall, facing eastward. Here the mountain rises precipitously, at an angle of over seventy degrees, toward the top of the pumice mountain, which towers four thousand feet higher. About eighty or one hundred feet up, a terrace gradually slopes back and is thickly covered with evergreen and undergrowth. The stream is only four or five feet wide at the fall, but below it spreads to fully twenty feet. (These particulars are reprinted for the benefit of "cement" hunters of the present day.) Camp made, Kent and McDougall cautiously crossed the great divide to the headwaters of Owens River. After searching, Kent identified certain landmarks and found a reddish ledge rich in free gold, though not very wide.

They took out gold to the amount of $40,000 that summer. They ran this into bars of about $2,000 each and distributed it among their packages when they moved out, in order to avoid exposing any of their treasure. When they left, they covered the marks of their work and hastened to San Francisco. Kent paid McDougall the money due him and transferred the bulk of the gold to Chicago. McDougall told how the secret work was continued until the summer of 1877, and declared that they took out each year from $25,000 to $50,000 worth of gold, amounting in all to from $350,000 to $400,000.

On the return of Kent and McDougall in 1877, Kent heard of the location of the Alpha and other claims at Mammoth and that a town was being built up. Satisfied that the whole country around there would soon swarm with prospectors, McDougall and Kent hastily secured as much gold as they could, thoroughly hid the traces of their work, and departed.

There is some speculation that Kent, the man McDougall had served, may have been Farnsworth come to collect the profits he had made from his discovery after murdering Hume and stealing his money. Whatever the case, McDougall wasn't telling exactly where they had dug, and Kent seems to have disappeared (in the same way Farnsworth had) after they eliminated all traces of the mine. It would seem that, once again, the mine was lost.

Even though the lost lode has never been found—that we know of for certain—many of the prospectors who flooded the Eastern Sierra looking for it did find gold, and lots of it. These other gold strikes resulted in the mining camps of Dogtown, Lundy Canyon, Mammoth City and many others. They also created what is said to be the most lawless town ever built: Bodie, California.

This marker lets people know that they are perhaps standing near their fortune—if they are lucky enough to find it.

The cement outcropping that became known as the Lost Cement Mine is said to lie somewhere in the dense woods near the Sierra Mountain headwaters of the Owens River. Even to this day, hopeful prospectors flock to the towns of Bishop or Mammoth and head out into the wilderness looking for what some say is the richest gold strike in history. For those thinking about a trip to find the lost mine, a good place to start is the Crestview Rest Area along Highway 395, fourteen miles north of Mammoth Lakes, California. A monument there states that somewhere nearby lies the Lost Cement Mine.

17

MONO LAKE

Mono Lake, now the largest lake wholly within the state of California, was once second in size only to its neighbor, Owens Lake. Both Mono and Owens Lakes have been decimated by the theft of their water by Los Angeles's Department of Water and Power. But that is where their similarities end. Owens Lake had clear, fresh water where fishing was abundant and steamships plied its surface. Mono Lake's water is salty, with an alkaline content so high that swimmers float with no effort and clothes are destroyed with prolonged exposure. Even with the high salinity, the beauty of this lake and surrounding shoreline is not diminished.

As acidic as the water is, Mono Lake is not bereft of life. While strolling along the shore of this inland lake, visitors will see millions of small, black flies milling about on the ground just out of reach of the lapping waves. Known as the Mono Lake alkali fly, these tiny critters are able to encase themselves in air bubbles, which allow them to walk underwater while looking for food and laying their eggs. During the summer months, the flies are so numerous that, when approached by people, they form an almost solid black cloud in their attempt to get away. These flies are a large part of the ecosystem and feed the large number of birds that call the lake home. These same flies were a major source of food for the Native Americans who lived along the lakeshore and islands.

The Kutzadika'a people are the predecessors of today's Mono Lake Paiute Native Americans. The actual origin of the name has been lost to time, at least among outsiders of the tribes. But it is believed to have come

The vast expanse of Mono Lake can be seen from the Conway Summit Scenic Overlook on Highway 395. Note how the highway leads directly to and along Mono Lake.

from the name the people called the fly pupae, *kutsavi*. It could be the Yokut Native American term for "fly eater." The Kutzadika'a people harvested the fly pupae during the summer, when the flies laid their eggs, and this was one of their main food sources to last them through the sometimes hard winters. As the name *Mono* is derived from the Yokut term *Monachi*, which is the name given to the tribes who live on both the west and east sides of the Sierra range, it is easy to see how the Mono tribe would have gotten its name.

The lake is also home to the Mono Lake brine shrimp. This shrimp is a food source for birds and other wildlife that flock to the lake during peak times. All life in and around Mono Lake is dependent on single-celled planktonic algae that reproduces rapidly during the winter and early spring because of runoff that brings high nutrients into the lake, which has no outlet. It is said that the lake can become as green as pea soup in years with an extremely high algae bloom. There are eight different worms that live in the sediment of the lake. Combined with the other life found in the waters of Mono Lake, these make up an ecosystem both complex and fragile.

When gold was discovered only a few miles from Mono Lake at Dogtown in 1857, and again in 1859 in nearby Monoville, settlers began to flock to the area in search of wealth. As they moved in and around the lake, the ecosystem began to deteriorate. Just a few years after the first discovery of the shiny metal, more than ten thousand people were living near the lake, and the Kutzadika'a were being pushed out. Where the Native people had been good stewards of the land and lake, the white man seemed as though he couldn't care less for the environment. Things slowly began to decline for Mono Lake.

In 1909, Wallis McPherson and his wife, Venita, moved into the Mono Basin. Wallis was employed by a local irrigation ditch company but spent his free time exploring the area and along the shores of Mono Lake. As he looked at the large, white island out in the lake, an idea came to his mind. Knowing that there were hot springs on the island, Pahoa, he thought it would make a great place to build a resort. To this end, McPherson purchased 350 acres on Pahoa and, with the help of an investor, another 135 acres on the mainland with plans to build a one-hundred-room hotel along the western shore of the lake and a "health resort" on the island. Wallis built a home for his family on Pahoa and had a boat shipped to Mono Lake via the Carson & Colorado Railroad that would transport his guests to the island spa. He named the boat *Pahoa*. Things were going well. A new bunkhouse and cookhouse were begun on the mainland when things took a sharp downward turn for McPherson. His investor passed away, and his heirs wanted nothing to do with a resort that was, in their words, "on the shore of a remote, desert lake." McPherson scaled back the hotel and used the bunkhouse, with six added rooms, as a small, intimate lodge and named it the Mono Inn. Wallis moved his family off the island and began using the *Pahoa* to take guests on lake excursions.

When Wallis and Venita divorced in 1926, Venita was awarded ownership of the Mono Inn and the *Pahoa* and was given custody of their son, Wally. With a lot of hard work, Venita and Wally turned the Mono Inn into a gathering place for locals and visitors alike. Writer Samuel Clemens wrote his classic book *Roughing It* and said that Mono Lake was a "solemn, sailless sea…little grace with the picturesque…with nothing that goes to make life desirable." But Venita used his disparaging words to her advantage and created Mark Twain Days. She held the event every August, and both locals and tourists attended with great fanfare. Things were looking good for Mono Lake tourism and for Venita, Wally and the area. But then Los Angles's thirst for water became like a vampire starving for blood.

As Los Angeles grew and its population increased, so did its need for water. The city had already been stealing the lifeblood of the Owens Valley

The Mono Inn during the winter season, with owner Vanita McPherson. *Courtesy of Mono Basin Historical Society.*

The Mono Inn is seen here during the peak of summer fishing season. *Courtesy of Mono Basin Historical Society.*

Shown here is an early occurrence of Mark Twain Days along Mono Lake. *Courtesy of Mono Basin Historical Society*

by diverting the river, but now, with the Owens Lake all but dry, Mono Lake began to be drained at an alarming rate. The water level dropped to the point that boating became too dangerous and the tufas became exposed, creating hazards to navigation. The marinas ceased to exist, Mono Inn closed and the lake began to dry up, just like its neighbor to the south. Los Angeles was killing Mono Lake, the ecosystem and the wildlife on a massive scale. The big city didn't seem to care; it was content to let Mono Lake and the entire Owens Valley die in order to satisfy its thirst. Luckily, in 1994, the California State Water Resources Control Board ordered the Los Angeles Department of Water and Power to return the water of Mono Lake to a level that would sustain ecological health and not only restore but also maintain that level in perpetuity. It has been decades since the ruling, and Mono Lake has still not reached the required water level. But it is almost there.

One of the things that makes Mono Lake one of the most beautiful lakes in California also makes it one of the most unusual. I am talking about the otherworldly looking tufas. With no natural outlet, the minerals, chemicals and other sediments flowing into Mono Lake have nowhere to go, so they build up on the lake bed until the water becomes saltier than the ocean. As springs along the bottom of the lake pump up calcium-rich water, the chemical reaction from salt, alkali and fresh water create stalagmites, or tufa towers, that slowly build and grow over time. Before the theft of the water, these tufa towers were completely submerged, but as the level of the lake declined, the tufas slowly came into view. Now, they stand above the waterline and, in some cases, well away from the shoreline, on dry land. These towers are a wonder to behold and create a landscape that resembles a faraway planet or a scene out of Dante's imagination.

The South Tufa Reserve is the best spot to view these wonders, and there is a marked trail that leads visitors along one of the most scenic areas of Mono Lake and offers views of some of the most picturesque tufas the lake has to offer. Although not found at the south reserve, there is one tufa that is a bit more unusual than most. It is not generally revealed where this tufa is located, for fear that vandals or careless individuals will damage it, much like

The many tufas, both in the lake and on the shoreline, give Mono Lake a landscape not seen anywhere else.

The "Icebox" tufa once had a bubbling spring inside. This helped keep the interior cool enough that early settlers used the tufa as a natural icebox in the hot Eastern Sierra summers.

they have other towers along the shoreline. This tufa not only has a distinct beauty to it but also had a functionality that helped settlers survive along the alkaline lake.

Early in the white settlers' time along Mono Lake, a woman by the name of Lily La Braque said that while living on the Nay Ranch, there was a large tufa that was hollow on the inside and big enough to not only step into but also store foodstuffs. The inside of this tufa, even in the hottest summer months, was at least twenty-five degrees cooler than the air outside. Because of this, the tufa was used to store eggs, butter and milk and on occasion meat to help keep these items from spoiling too quickly. The ranch is no longer there, having been swallowed up by the rising lake water after the 1906 San Francisco earthquake, but the Icebox Tufa of Mono Lake, as it has become known, is still there.

18

BODIE GHOST TOWN

Like its southern neighbor Cerro Gordo, the ghost town of Bodie in northeast California, right off Highway 395, is considered one of the top five ghost towns in the country to visit. One of the reasons for this is that, when California turned it into a state historic park in 1962, authorities decided that the buildings should be kept as they were. That is not to say that the state doesn't maintain the structures and area, only that the town is kept in what is called a "state of arrested decay."

This hands-off approach to preservation allows visitors to both see and feel what it must have been like in those last days when the town was being abandoned and folks up and left, leaving most if not all of their belongings behind. In Bodie, guests can wander a bit into many of the buildings and see furniture, utensils and canned food products, as well as photos, bedding and even clothing, all left behind by those who called Bodie home. Abandoned bars left behind in the exodus still have glassware and booze bottles, newspaper offices still have their presses and even a funeral parlor remains, replete with unused coffins still standing in the window display. All of this and more can be found here, thanks to the state's minimal intrusion on history.

The town was founded around 1860 after a small band of prospectors, drawn to the area by the lure of the gold rush, wandered through a valley near Mono Lake in 1858. One of these men was W.S. Bodey. There is still some confusion regarding Bodey's name. In some histories, his name is written as William, in others as Wakeman. The four men discovered a

The ghost town of Bodie looks like it could eventually fade from view. But the State of California maintains the town in what it calls a "state of arrested decay."

gold strike in the valley, set up their claim and began pulling gold from the earth. As winter drew near, the men realized that they would need supplies to see them through to spring. Bodey and his partner E.S. "Black" Taylor left on the supply run. Unfortunately, on the return trip, they were caught in a severe snowstorm. Taylor managed to make it back to camp with the supplies, but Bodey, unfortunately, perished. His corpse was lost for twenty years following his death, and he was buried where his remains were eventually found.

Legend has it that, after Bodey's body was located, the town of Bodie collected donations for a monument in his honor. It is said that the monument was to be used as a cenotaph for President James Garfield, who had recently died, but was repurposed for Bodey. The name on the monument refers to him as William S. Bodey.

W.S. Bodey's name has even been elevated to legendary status, not from the town that took his name but from the many different names that he has been known by, or called, before and after his death. Besides the two names mentioned above, Bodey was also referred to as Wateman, Waterman, Waitman, Whitman, Waiteman and Bill. It is not only his first name that is mired in controversy but also his last name.

It is said that the name of the town, Bodie, came as the result of a sign painter for the town who did not like the spelling of Bodey. He believed that the spelling we know today was harder to mispronounce and more appealing to the eye. He took his thoughts to the townsfolk, who readily agreed. The town's name and spelling thus became Bodie. This is the legend, anyway. However, while Bodey was alive, he was known by several last names, not unlike his many given names. Other surnames and spellings he went by included Body, Boddy, Boda and Bodie. In the *Kitchell Family History*, an 881-page genealogy (Gregath Company, 1989), the author lists his birth and death dates and names him as Waiteman Supple Bodie. Even the family Bible lists Bodey and Boddy, further complicating what the true family name might have been.

The first claim at Bodie, the Montauk, began producing gold almost immediately. But as the discovery came about at roughly the same time as the Comstock lode was just getting started, interest in the Bodie area remained light. As word trickled in regarding the harsh conditions in and around Bodie, as well as reports of minimal production, it wasn't until 1875, after a massive cave-in at one of the mines had exposed a large ore vein, that attention was finally given to the failing town. The town began to grow, and within two years the population had reached four thousand miners and townsfolk.

Claims began to be purchased by investment groups, and mills began to spring up to handle the large amounts of gold finally being pulled from the earth. In 1877, the Standard Company alone reported $784,523 in gold and silver ore pulled from its claims. This made the company's investors extremely happy, and they authorized the construction of a new stamp mill. This mill still stands at Bodie today, and its inner workings are still mostly intact.

The Standard strike, coupled with another large find the following year, brought more fortune seekers to the town, and investors came with them. The winter of 1878–79 was particularly harsh, and many people who came to Bodie during that time died of exposure for want of proper housing. And with mining accidents a common occurrence in the rush to secure the ore, along with the wealth that came with it, many more perished as a result. Even with these hardships, by 1880, Bodie had grown to a population of roughly ten thousand people, with approximately two thousand structures spread out within the valley and thirty mines pulling ore out of the countryside. To serve the growing population, Bodie sported three newspapers, a post office, three breweries, a Chinatown with opium dens, several gambling halls, quite a few brothels, a brass band and sixty-five saloons. What the town didn't have was a single house of worship. The first church wasn't built until 1882, and even then, only two existed in a town of ten thousand people.

Because Bodie was situated in a desert landscape, wood was not readily available. Almost everything a mining town uses requires wood, from buildings to mine shoring. Wood is the one commodity a town like Bodie cannot do without. Because of this need, massive amounts of lumber had to be carted in daily from the Sierra. The Chinese living at Bodie shipped it in by the wagonload. The Chinese population of Bodie was indispensable for everyday life in the town. They worked as household servants; washed clothing for the townsfolk; performed cheap, manual labor around town; and were even responsible for evening entertainment, with several gambling halls and opium dens spread throughout Chinatown. They were also instrumental in the building of the Bodie & Benton Railroad. When this line was completed, the trains brought in approximately one hundred thousand cords of wood each year. To keep the wood coming into town, the Bodie & Benton needed a steady workforce. Once again, the railroad turned to the cheap Chinese labor force. With unemployment on the rise in the mines, this angered quite a few of the townsfolk, and fights broke out among the miners and the Chinese. Fighting and murder, however, were not uncommon occurrences in Bodie.

It is said that Bodie was one of the largest towns in California, second only to San Francisco. While San Francisco was considered a growing, sophisticated, metropolitan city, Bodie had a reputation as anything but a civilized town. After long days working in the mines, and with many miners being single, the first thing these lonely men would do after work was hit the many bars and opium dens found throughout the town. Loneliness and alcohol are never a good combination, and fights broke out among the miners, sometimes over the "Soiled Doves" the men were vying for, at other times over gambling losses or sometimes just because. Many of these fights ended in bloodshed and death. With the amount of gold, silver and other valuable ores coming from the mines, bandits were drawn to Bodie in the hopes that the drunks would be easy pickings. Gunfights, shootings and murderous brawls became a nightly occurrence. These crimes became so prevalent that town newspapers began reporting that people would ask over their morning meal, "Have we a man for breakfast?" The meaning of this was said to be, "Did anyone get killed last night?" The answer was generally, "yes."

Bodie was second in size only to San Francisco and was considered the roughest town in America. *Courtesy of Mono County Historical Society.*

Bodie's reputation around the country was so bad that tales of its debauchery were found in newspapers far and wide. Common descriptors of the town were found in comments such as "a sea of sin, lashed by a tempest of lust and passion," and "the worst climate out of doors that one can imagine." One of the worst comments, possibly anecdotal, was a news piece stating that a young girl moving to Bodie with her family wrote in her diary, "Goodbye God, I'm going to Bodie." A tale was even invented for parents to frighten their children into behaving: the "bad man of Bodie" would get them if they were naughty.

These reports and stories still did not deter folks from all over the country and around the world from coming to Bodie to seek their fortunes. A report in the *Daily Bodie Standard* reported, "The stages come in loaded with passengers and leave loaded with bullion." People coming into town had dreams of being the one to find the "mother lode" that everyone knew was just about to show itself to some lucky miner. Every day, men ventured into their claims, and every night, those same men trudged home disappointed. By the late 1880s, it started to become clear that there was no mother lode to be found, and mines began to close up as their operators went looking for opportunities elsewhere.

A few of the larger mining endeavors, those with good financial backing, remained in operation. There was just not enough work for the many miners who remained in town. Looking at another harsh winter with no job, and hearing about new strikes in other states, many miners packed up and headed with their families for greener pastures. By 1892, the population of Bodie had dwindled to just around eight hundred people. In that same year, a fire broke out, destroying a large portion of the town. This caused another mass exodus from Bodie.

The dominoes continued to fall after the fire, and despite the fact that the country's first long-distance electrical transmission plant was built in nearby Bridgeport to serve Bodie, the town was dying. In 1914, James S. Cain purchased the largest operation in Bodie, the Standard Mine, and as much property as he could in the hopes of saving the town. In 1915, the Standard produced a $100,000 profit, but by 1917, the mine was all but played out. The new power plant had been destroyed in an avalanche in 1911. And the Bodie & Benton Railroad (now the Mono Lake Railway and Lumber Company) had its tracks removed and sold for scrap, and the company closed down in 1915. Bodie's days were numbered.

Even though the town continued to survive, the 1920 census placed its population at only 120 souls. Bodie had already become a ghost town, and now folks were actually calling it such. The final nail in the coffin of the town came in 1932. Legend has it that a toddler known as "Bodie Bill," upset that he didn't have a birthday cake, set his house on fire. The fire spread, and with so few people left to battle it, most of the remaining town went up in flames. After the fire, the only ones who remained at Bodie were the employees still working at the Roseklip Mine. However, when World War II began, the federal government stepped in and ordered all mining operations at Bodie to cease. Those persons remaining in the town packed up, leaving the town abandoned.

With the town completely uninhabited, the Cains, who were still the primary owners of Bodie, began to fear that vandals and vagrants would move in and either damage or destroy the remaining buildings. The Cain family knew the historic importance of Bodie, and to make sure the town was looked after and kept safe, they hired caretakers to oversee and maintain the structures in the old mining town. The family began looking into turning Bodie over to the state and finally deeded the town and the land to the State of California. In 1962, Bodie was designated a California State Park and in that same year was added to the National Register of Historic Places. Two years later, the town was dedicated as Bodie State

Historic Park and is now overseen by rangers of the California State Department of Parks and Recreation.

For those traveling along Highway 395, Bodie can be reached by turning on to State Route 270 and driving down a thirteen-mile-long road, only ten miles of which are paved. This road is usually closed during the harsh winter months. The town is most definitely worth the trip, but there are a couple of things to be on the lookout for.

The first is the fact that the town is haunted. The Cain House and the Mendocini, Gregory and Dechambeau Houses all have their fair share of reported ghost activity. Even along the streets and alleyways in the evening, spirits have been both seen and heard by visitors and rangers alike. None of the spirits at Bodie are malicious or violent; they appear to be going about their business as if they don't know they have passed, or they may love the town so much that it will always be home to them. Besides, it is not the spirits of the town one must be wary of; it is the town's curse you must steer clear of. Luckily, that is easy to do.

The "Curse of Bodie Ghost Town" is believed by many to have been created by the rangers tasked with preserving the town. Having visitors

Bodie in its heyday was known for its bars, brothels and shootouts. *Courtesy of Mono County Historical Society.*

Today, due to fire and economics, Bodie is but a shell of what it once was.

pick up nails or pieces of metal laying on the ground or other artifacts that are now a part of the town and taking them home as souvenirs would have caused Bodie to slowly disappear. Bodie would then only be remembered by those people who selfishly hoard the pieces in their home. Even stones and pebbles from the town are picked up and carried away. This is where the curse comes in.

It is said that anyone taking a piece of the town from Bodie will be struck with such bad luck that their lives will be turned upside down. Only by returning the stolen item will the bad luck be removed and life returned to normal. Sounds like a good story for the rangers to tell to keep guests from removing pieces of the town, doesn't it? There is one problem with the theory that the tale is made up, and that is that there is evidence the curse may be real.

Inside the museum and store at Bodie, the State of California keeps a ledger of all of the things that have been returned by those who have both consciously taken items and those who have inadvertently picked up a rock lodged in the tread of a shoe or a bag carelessly set down where something could fall into it. Packages with nails, bits of scrap, colored stones and common rocks have all been sent by mail, UPS, FedEx and hand-delivered back to town by those desperate to redeem their lives from what they have called "a living hell." There are stories of car crashes, job losses, broken marriages and even death associated with the Curse of Bodie. So prevalent has the curse become that many TV documentaries about the town now place the curse as a prominent part of the narratives. So, when visiting Bodie, just keep your eyes open and your bags shut, and check your shoes before driving off.

PART III

WEIRD AND WILD SIERRA

19

CRYPTIDS OF THE SIERRA MOUNTAINS

THE LONE PINE MOUNTAIN DEVIL

Some have said that the Lone Pine Mountain Devil is the West Coast cousin of the New Jersey Devil. The similarities in behavior, appearance and elusiveness make this a plausible theory, but as there are few firsthand accounts of what the actual creature looks like, one cannot say conclusively either way. What we do know is that the Lone Pine Devil has supposedly been around since the Spanish began colonizing California. I say "supposedly," because there is also the possibility that this cryptid is nothing more than an elaborate internet hoax.

First reported by a Spanish padre who walked out of the wilderness of the Owens Valley after his wagon train was attacked by the beast, Father Justus Martinez told those at the mission when he arrived that all of the people he was traveling with had been eaten by a lizard-like creature with wings. The monster had eaten only the settlers' torsos and had devoured all thirty-six human beings in one meal. Martinez said that the only reason he survived was because he had camped away from the group while the creature went about its evil work. The padre thought that the creature acted in retribution for the burning of the forest trees in the campfires.

There had been no sightings of the Lone Pine Mountain Devil since 1928, and some folks reasoned that it was due to the influx of people moving to the area as well as tourists passing through, or the fact that the water was stolen from the Owens Valley. Whatever the reason, the reports all but stopped until the early 2000s.

With the rise of the internet, sightings of this creature again began to pour in. Reports of people mysteriously disappearing from the Alabama Hills, Death Valley and Whitney Portal, as well as from the peak itself, became common internet fodder. This has spawned the idea that the creature itself is nothing more than a creation of the World Wide Web being fed by imagination and creative writing. Whatever the case may be—truth, fiction or a combination of the two—I leave this up to my intrepid readers. This I will say: beware and be on the lookout for this elusive monster of Owens Valley lore…just in case!

High Sierra Sasquatch

Bigfoot sightings have become well known these days. Television shows, tabloid news and daytime talk shows flood the airwaves for whatever ratings they can get, and Bigfoot reports have almost become commonplace. With Highway 395 running between the Sierra Range on the west and the Panamint Mountains on the east, it should come as no surprise that there would be plenty of Sasquatch tales along the El Camino Sierra.

I spoke with the folks at the Sierra Strange Museum and gift shop, and they told me about what they called the Crowley Lake, or Glass Mountain, Bigfoot. The story goes that at dawn one fine spring day, a fisherman was out on his boat, his line in the water and enjoying the beautiful scenery along the lake. As he surveyed the shoreline across from him, he noticed what at first he assumed was a bear feeding on fish. He watched as the bear used his hands to snatch a fish from the water and hungrily start eating it. That is when he remembered that bears have paws, not hands. As he watched, the creature finished its meal, stood up and looked over at the stunned fisherman. Just before the creature wandered back into the forest, the Sasquatch—for that is what the man realized it was—raised its chin, gave an odd grunt at him and disappeared. The man debated telling anyone about what he had seen but decided it was too good a story to not relate.

About a month after the fisherman sighted the Bigfoot, a family was camping on the lake. While fixing dinner, they heard some rustling behind their campsite. Thinking it might be a bear or some other dangerous animal, the family locked themselves in their car. Looking out from the windows, they saw a very large, hairy humanoid wander through camp, looking around and sniffing their food. The creature glanced at the family locked in their car, tilted its head at them and wandered out of sight. The family stayed in their car for a while and then quickly packed up and headed home.

Lake Crowley isn't the only place along the 395 that Bigfoot has been seen. There is a Paiute legend that says an entire family of Sasquatch lives in Walker Canyon and that they are very protective of their home. Native American lore tells of how the Sasquatch will keep watch on travelers as they pass through and will leave them alone as long as they respect the Bigfoot's home. Those who disrespect it will find the creatures angry, even hostile, if the visitors are destructive. Other legends say that a friendly, symbiotic relationship has occurred, with Native Americans leaving fish and other foodstuff for the Sasquatch, who in turn leave meat that they have caught, along with wild nuts and berries, for the Paiute who have been kind to them. Campers in the area have been reporting Bigfoot sightings in Walker Canyon for many years. Sightings have also been reported around the tourist area of Twin Lakes just outside of the town of Bridgeport.

Also just outside of Bridgeport is an old, abandoned mining camp reached by driving up Masonic Road. Many ATV enthusiasts use this area for recreation and exploration. A few years ago, a couple riding along the trail began to hear what they described as a "chirping sound" coming from all around them. Not knowing what was making the noise, they stopped and shut off their motors to see if the sound was coming from one of their machines. It was not, and now the couple could hear that the sound was coming from many places and almost seemed as if it was a communication among many creatures. As they stood listening, they began to see tall, hairy, humanoid figures all around them, looking at them. They realized that they had somehow wandered into a group of Sasquatches. They immediately started their ATVs and hightailed it out of the area.

There are many other tales of Sasquatch being seen up and down Highway 395, from the Lone Pine area up past the Nevada border. Campers and hikers come out of the mountains with tales of run-ins with these elusive creatures, and Native American lore from the area is filled with stories about the creature—tales of both good and ill. When driving along the 395 or venturing into the lush wilderness, keep an eye out for Bigfoot and treat it with caution and kindness, for it may return this in kind.

SKINWALKERS OF THE 395

When skinwalkers are talked about, most people think of Skinwalker Ranch, possible space aliens and portals to other dimensions. Most of these tales are fiction for mass media consumption and may not have much basis in true legends and lore of Native Americans. Be that as it may, while talking with those at the Sierra Strange Museum, I was told about an old Paiute woman who lived near Bridgeport, just off Highway 395, who had been stalked by a skinwalker her entire life.

For those who may not be familiar with skinwalkers, they are a legend of most Native American tribes. They are said to be the original shape-shifters, even pre-dating werewolves and other lycanthropes. Skinwalkers, unlike Sasquatches, are not known for their benevolent behavior. They are, in most cases, vicious, cruel creatures. Keeping this in mind, one can see why someone would dread a lifetime of being followed by one of them.

The story says that this woman first discovered the skinwalker when she was a child and that as she grew up she felt its presence watching her as she went about her chores. Over the years, it would get closer to her, and she began to fear for her safety. It followed her for her entire life, but it never seemed to do more than threaten and scare her. After she had a family of her own, the skinwalker began to take notice of her husband and children. This scared her more than being followed herself. She went often to the shamans, and they would attempt to get it to leave her alone. But nothing worked. After the woman passed away, her son and family began talking to the tribal elders and shamans to tell them that the skinwalker was now following and stalking them. To this day, the family says that they feel the gaze of the skinwalker on them and can sense it keeping an eye on their every move.

With eerie, otherworldly landscapes along Highway 395, it is not hard to imagine skinwalkers and demon donkeys wandering its roadsides.

This could easily be just a legend of the area, but many visitors have reported seeing a creature that will look like a man one minute, then suddenly change into a bear, a wolf or another menacing animal. Could this be a product of imagination brought on by shadows from the fading sunlight and a long day exploring the wilderness near Bridgeport? Or could the skinwalkers exist and be more widespread and less confined—more than just the phenomena of Skinwalker Ranch?

Demonio Burro

The Demon Donkey is a piece of lore that grew up near the town of Coso Junction along Highway 395. This Mexican tale is that of a donkey who appears to weary travelers and tries to lead them down to hell. The donkey is a pet of Lucifer himself and has been tasked with bringing souls to the underworld. In the 1800s, those traveling through the area who began to tire and despair would be greeted by a friendly donkey. This donkey would then lead the weary wanderer to what they thought was a place to rest for the night. In reality, the burro was leading them off a precipice or into a pack of wild coyotes, wolves or bears. The demise was always different, but the outcome was always death and an eternity in hell. Although people no longer travel by horse and wagon or walk hundreds of miles through the Owens Valley, the tale of the Demonio Burro persists to this day, albeit the donkey has changed its tactics.

The proprietor of Sierra Strange related that he and a friend may have almost become victims of the Demon Donkey. He said that while driving through Coso Junction one night on their way to Mammoth, he and his friend were marveling at the strange lunar landscape that surrounds the highway in this area, made more surreal by the last of the day's light. They rounded a slight curve, and there, in the middle of the roadway, stood a burro. They had to slam on the brakes to avoid hitting the animal. At the speed they were traveling, and with what he said was an abnormally large donkey, the two men may not have survived impact with the animal.

After the car came to a screeching halt and the men regained the ability to breathe normally, they looked around for the donkey, but it had already vanished. When they calmed down enough to drive, they continued on to Mammoth to meet up with his wife, Candy.

Candy at that time worked at the Old New York Deli in Mammoth, and one of her fellow employees, a Mexican gentleman, overheard the story and told them the legend of the Demon Burro. They had never heard the tale before. But after encountering a burro—rare along Highway 395—and considering the fact that after the accident the burro was nowhere to be found, they wondered if indeed they had run into Diablo Burro, as Candy's coworker suggested.

Whether the Diablo Burro is just a tale or truth, while driving the El Camino Sierra, keep an eye open for a lone donkey, and give it a wide berth—just in case.

20

SILVER AND GHOSTS, SILVER AND GHOSTS...

OWENS LAKE AND THE LEGEND OF THE BESSIE BRADY

Today, Owens Lake is nothing more than a small puddle in a giant salt flat that was, at one time, one of the largest lakes in California. The City of Los Angeles, in its gluttonous quest for water, decided that its need was greater than the needs of those living in the Owens Valley and turned this once lush, beautiful farmland into the dust bowl we see today.

When the lake was still a full and vibrant water source along the now almost nonexistent Owens River, it played an important role in the development of the surrounding area. One doesn't usually associate steamboats with lake travel, but the Owens Lake and its "Desert Steamers"—the *Bessie Brady* and the *Mollie Stevens*—became part of local lore. The *Bessie Brady* would also give life to a legend of riches that still lives on to this day.

Silver ore came flooding down from the mines of Cerro Gordo to the smelters in the town of Swansea, was formed into bars, transported around the lake and finally shipped down to Los Angeles. As a result, ideas were forming to find ways to shorten the trip. The answer came from James Brady, the superintendent and, some say, dandy of the Owens Lake Silver-Lead Company in Swansea. Brady commissioned a steamer to be built, and the keel was laid at the end of February 1872. Such was the man's reputation for being a snobby easterner that most people believed Brady was building a personal lake yacht using company funds. The steamer had its maiden voyage on June 27, carrying seven hundred bars of silver from the Swansea furnaces to wagons waiting for it on the other side of the lake.

After the steamer successfully completed its maiden voyage, it was tied up at the dock for another week while the shipwrights completed its deckhouses and other minor details. On July 4, 1872, during the area's Independence Day celebration, the new steamer was christened *Bessie Brady*. Christening aside, it would still take until the end of July for the steamer to be completely fitted and ready to begin its career and secure its place in history.

The ship needed a safe and deep place to offload the silver bullion, so construction began on a wharf in what would become the town of Cartago on the west side of the lake. By early August 1872, it had been completed and was ready for use. The *Bessie Brady* began making regular crossings of Owens Lake, transporting silver bars from the Swansea furnaces to the docks at Cartago. The vessel would then be loaded up with charcoal to deliver to Swansea on the return trip. Taking the ore over the lake by ship was so successful that the wagon teams that had been tramping through the muddy ground along the lakeshore heading to the road to Los Angeles were discontinued. James Brady's idea was a complete success.

Unfortunately, there are times when something can become a victim of its own success, and the *Bessie Brady* became a good example of this. Making

Shown here is all that is left of the once proud *Bessie Brady*.

more than one trip across Owens Lake daily, the *Bessie Brady* could transport the bullion as fast as Swansea could form it into bars. The problem was that, once the silver was offloaded at Cartago, it still had to be moved down to Los Angeles by horse-drawn wagons. As the trip was a two-hundred-mile journey each way, the silver ingots began to pile up on the docks as it was delivered. There was such a backlog that by January 1873, there were 181,000 silver bars piled up on the docks, in the streets of Cartago and even along the shoreline. A total of $600,000 was stacked and awaiting shipment south.

The delay in the delivery of the silver caused the Owens Lake Silver-Lead Company to shut down and lay off workers. Those employed at the docks had no work, and the *Bessie Brady* was tied up at the eastern wharf and sitting idle. It got to be so bad that some of the unemployed persons stacked up the unshipped silver bars and used them as makeshift housing.

Seeing an opportunity, one of Cerro Gordo's principal mine owners got together with a Los Angeles teamster and formed the Cerro Gordo Freighting Company. They bought out all of the other shipping companies, expanded to forty-six teams running freight and began hauling the ore from Cartago. Each wagon team carried an average of 170 bars, and the bullion stacks were finally beginning to dwindle. As the stacks of silver bars grew smaller on the docks, the smelting furnaces started up, the shipments started rolling out again and the *Bessie Brady* was once more plying the waters of the lake.

In June 1877, the *Bessie Brady* was joined on the lake by its smaller, more powerful sister, the *Mollie Stevens*. This steamer was operated by a rival company, but both companies managed to stay peaceful rivals. In fact, during an early *Stevens* voyage, the *Bessie Brady* was called to tow and raise the *Stevens* from the lake bottom when it swamped and sank.

As mining activity in the area was on the decline, the *Mollie Stevens* began to make fewer lake crossings. By the end of 1878, it was tied up at the Cottonwood pier and spent its time idle. The *Bessie Brady* was soon to follow.

When Captain Julius Keeler arrived in the Owens Valley in 1879 with plans to build a ten-stamp mill at the foot of the "Yellow Grade Road" from Cerro Gordo, it looked like things might turn around for the inland steamers. After the ground-breaking for the mill at what would become the town of Keeler, the new firm, the Owens Lake Mining and Milling Company, bought up a number of mines in Cerro Gordo, along with the Cottonwood sawmill and flume; this purchase included the steamers *Mollie Stevens* and *Bessie Brady*. Being the newer ship, the *Mollie Stevens* was brought out of retirement. But despite being a younger ship, it lacked stamina. It wasn't long before the

Stevens was again retired, its engines mated to the *Bessie Brady*, which was in the process of being completely overhauled.

Unfortunately, the resurgence of the Owens Valley steamers was not to be. On May 11, 1882, with the work on the *Bessie Brady* nearly complete, a fire broke out from the tar, oil and paint storage area. The *Bessie Brady* was turned into a raging mass of flames. The age of the inland steamers was over, and little remains of the *Bessie Brady* other than a beacon light preserved in the town of Independence and an enduring legend of lost silver waiting to be found in the salt of the Owens Dry Lake.

The legend of the lost silver of the Owens Lake is one of the most well-known and enduring tales of the Owens Valley. The legend began in November 1875, when, on a windy winter evening, the *Bessie Brady* was completing its final transit of the day. The story was told by a W.G. Dixon, who heard it from Ned Smith, the captain of the steamer when the incident occurred. Smith said that as they approached the middle of the lake, the wind whipped so hard that the waves were growing fierce. The *Bessie Brady* was getting tossed about. Smith wasn't worried about the steamer floundering, but one of the two wagons filled with silver ingots hadn't been sufficiently chained down and was coming loose. Before the crew could secure the wagon, the boat pitched, sending the wagon toward the water of the lake. The crew managed to catch the cart before it toppled, but not before some of the silver bullion was lost. Dixon said of Ned Smith, "The man is a verbal novelist and his story is probably no more than pure fiction."

Fiction or fact, the legend lives on today, with many locals retelling the tale to travelers and out-of-town visitors armed with not only fishing poles and camping equipment but also metal detectors, waterproof boots and high hopes of striking it rich by finding the Lost Owens Lake Treasure. Who knows, maybe one day someone will prove W.G. Dixon's assessment of Ned Smith wrong. However, for now, the lost silver of Owens Valley will remain a legend.

LONE PINE GHOSTS

It is not just movie sites, camping spots and artwork that can be found in the Alabama Hills. There are some things more sinister, and perhaps evil, that legend has it live within the peaceful hills around Lone Pine.

The once vast Owens Lake was the site of a battle between the Owens Valley Paiute Nation and U.S. troops. It is said that the sights and sounds of this battle can be heard to this day.

It is said that the sounds of a long-past battle that took place between the U.S. Army and Native Paiute people can still be heard while driving along Whitney Portal Road. This road, the only one that crosses Highway 395 with a traffic light in the small town, passes right through the battleground. In the many years since homes were constructed along the route, people have reported hearing the sounds of gunfire, screams of agony and the sound of men clashing. It is said that one woman looked out of her window to see a Paiute warrior looking back at her. The warrior ignored her as he rushed off toward the sounds of the raging battle. Many people assume that ghostly activity comes only in the dark of night, but the people in this area hear the sounds of warfare both day and night. There seems to be no rhyme or reason as to when the spirits begin their fight, but many locals have become accustomed to the sounds.

There have also been reports, albeit not for many years, of a full-on ghostly battle that takes place between Native Americans and U.S. Cavalry along the shores of Owens Lake. Those telling the tale say that both Paiute and U.S. soldiers can be seen falling from their horses and being trampled by the animals. All of them, men and horses, look as real and solid as everything else around them. The strange thing about this story is that the description of what those people had seen coincides exactly with a battle that took place there many years earlier.

Another Paiute man has been seen near upper Whitney Portal Road. This Native American, however, is not engaged in battle but is instead on the lookout for travelers in need of aid. Indian Jim, or as some call him, Rescue Man, has become a local legend since his death in the 1940s. This prospector who froze to death in a sudden blizzard has now taken it upon himself to warn people roaming the Alabama Hills about incoming severe storms. Jim will approach those who need warning, just close enough to be heard, and point toward Lone Pine while uttering a single word: "Go." Jim has saved many people just before deadly rain or snowstorms have hit the area. If you see this kindly soul, it is recommended that you heed his warning.

The Dow Villa Hotel/Motel in the heart of Lone Pine is said to be haunted. This historic hotel/motel directly along Highway 395 was built in the 1920s for the Hollywood celebrities coming to Lone Pine to film in the Alabama Hills. It would seem that some of its past guests decided to remain.

The Best Western Plus Frontier Hotel on 395 as you enter town from the south also has a resident ghost. It is said that, early in the mornings, a man in a cowboy hat can be seen in the rooms or strolling down the walkways of the hotel.

Bridgeport and the White Lady

Bridgeport, California, is one of those towns along Highway 395 that you drive through on your way to somewhere else, or perhaps make a quick stop for gas or a bite to eat. Seldom does one think to themselves, "Hey, let's go to Bridgeport." Unless, that is, you are a fisherman. I was the same way, just passing through, until one day I decided to walk around this little town and found out there is more to Bridgeport than meets the eye.

In August 1860, silver was found south of the great Comstock Lode of Nevada, and prospectors flocked to the area in search of fortune. As the site was so near the border of California and Nevada, no one was quite sure which state they were actually in. Because of this, those in the area declared themselves to be part of the Golden State. A new town quickly grew, with an eight-stamp mill, which was called Pioneer. By 1861, more than two thousand people had come to live in the town of Aurora. The people of the Bridgeport Valley and surrounding area petitioned the state to create Mono County, and Aurora became the county seat. There was one problem. After the "Sage Brush Survey" of 1863 found that Aurora was actually just across the border in Nevada, California immediately chose the town of Bridgeport as the new seat of Mono County. The Bridgeport Courthouse, a masterpiece of Italianate elegance, has stood there since April 1881 and today is the second-oldest continually active courthouse in California.

Another building that distinguishes itself in town with its Victorian style and charm is the Bridgeport Inn. The inn was built in 1877 as the private residence of Hiram Leavitt. Hiram contracted Sam Hopkins to build his dream house. After its completion, Leavitt and his family lived in the home until Hiram's death in 1901. Hopkins, having spent quite a bit of time around the Leavitt family while constructing their house, fell in love with Hiram's daughter Ida and married her after the house was finished. At some point between the time the house was finished in 1877 and 1887, Hiram turned his home into an inn. With scores of people traveling through Bridgeport headed to Bodie and other gold-mining areas, Leavitt had decided to capitalize on the influx of travelers. His decision would have a lasting effect on not only the inn but also the town.

Gold rush merchant A. McGillvray, known simply as Mac, and his fiancée, Sarah, arrived in Bridgeport after traveling from Bodie. They checked into the inn for the night, but as Mac was continuing on to Carson City the following day to pick up parts for the new hydroelectric plant being built to power Bodie, he would be gone for three days. Sarah would be staying at the inn until his return. The commission Mac was to make on the delivery would allow the couple to realize their dream of making a life for themselves in the town of Sonora, California. Mac and Sarah were deeply in love and planned to be married as soon as he arrived back in Bridgeport. Neither wanted to be away from each other, but the thought of their nuptials was enough to keep them happy, if not content, until they were reunited.

Mac had asked the Leavitts to watch over his beloved, and the family promised to treat her as one of their own. Sarah's wedding dress was being sewn by a seamstress in Bridgeport, and since Sarah was staying in town, it had been arranged for the final fitting to be done the day after she checked into the inn. After the dress was complete, Sarah carefully hung it up in the wardrobe and then spent a pleasant afternoon at the Jim Cain cabin along nearby Virginia Lake. Once back at the inn, Sarah was invited to a

The Bridgeport Inn is said to be haunted by the White Lady. A stay in this historic inn should be on everyone's list when traveling Highway 395.

family feast of venison, followed by an evening recital on the patio given by the Leavitts' daughter Amanda. As Sarah lay down to sleep, she smiled, thinking about the wonderful day she had had and the magical wedding and life to come.

Sometime around midnight, Sarah was awoken by loud voices coming from downstairs. She couldn't make out what was being said but knew by the tone that it was dire. A few minutes later, Hiram Leavitt was knocking on her door and asked her to come to the parlor. The entire Leavitt family was there. They asked her to sit down, and with a sinking feeling, she did as asked. In a solemn tone, Hiram told Sarah that while on the way to Carson City, Mac's wagon and the stagecoach had been robbed and that he, along with the three Wells Fargo guards who had gone along to protect a shipment of gold on the wagon, had been shot and killed. The stagecoach and wagon driver had escaped and hurried back to get help to form a posse to search for the robbers. Sarah was devastated at the news and had to be helped back to her room by Amanda Leavitt, who stayed with the grieving woman through the night.

The next day, Sarah dressed herself in her newly completed wedding dress and wandered the inn in a despondent fugue. The family tried to help,

The White Lady is mostly seen in what was once her room, now room 16. But she is also seen frequently descending the stairway leading up to the hotel area of the Bridgeport Inn.

but no one knew what to say or do to ease the young woman's pain. They could only watch and pray for her. Sarah's life was shattered, her dreams gone. As she sat in her room, she knew she couldn't go on without the love of her life. Sometime during the night, Amanda went to check on the young woman, and when she entered Sarah's room, she found her friend hanging from a rope, dead. On the table next to her bed a note was found that read: "Mac was my only love, my partner for life. I wait for him here, where we last shared our dreams. Now I will love him for eternity as his wife."

Mac and Sarah were buried together in Sonora on their planned wedding day in December. Sarah, however, may not have stayed with her beloved. It is said by the Bridgeport Inn staff and guests that Sarah, the "White Lady," as she has come to be known, is still at the inn. She has been seen in the hallways, on the stairs and mostly in room 16, which was the room Sarah lived and died in.

Bridgeport is the county seat, and a historic one at that. It may also be one of the most haunted places along Highway 395. The Bridgeport Inn may not be the only haunted spot in town. The Bodie Hotel, one of the oldest buildings in Bridgeport, is said to have its fair share of spirits. Guests have reported their belongings being moved around and taken even while they were in the room. Guests have reported seeing misty figures in the rooms, in the lobby and on the stairs. The 1881 house at the north end of town has had so many reports that it would take more words than this chapter will allow to describe them, and the old town jail is said to still be occupied by past criminals and miscreants forever awaiting trial at the courthouse.

Perhaps the most famous Beat Generation author, Jack Kerouac, stayed at the Bridgeport Inn while he and a couple of friends climbed Matterhorn Peak in nearby Groveland, California. He dedicated forty pages to the town and his adventures here in his book *The Dharma Bums*. So, when driving along Highway 395 into Bridgeport, instead of just passing through and getting a brief glimpse of this little town, stop, look around, talk to the townsfolk and enjoy the quaint charm and peacefulness of this historic, tranquil slice of California history.

EPILOGUE

When I began driving this road, it was only to travel to the lights and casinos of Reno or, more often, to the historic and haunted town of Virginia City, Nevada. I was just driving through and not really paying attention. Once, I drove through the concentration camp, colloquially called a "relocation camp," and I began to realize how much I was missing. I decided to pay attention. It was the beginning of a journey that seemingly has no end.

Every time I drive the El Camino Sierra, I find a new piece of history, a new legend and new tales of wondrous lore that fill this area of California. There are tales of mining towns in the middle of nowhere, accessible only by foot, that were once thriving communities. There are stories of pioneers who have unceremoniously made our lives richer for their being alive yet are known by few for their accomplishments, such as George Ferris. He invented the Ferris wheel, which most of us have or will enjoy. There were the women who bucked the misogynistic ideals of the time to become forerunners of a movement still going today. And there were the simple men and women who, just living their lives the best way they knew how, made all of our lives richer.

This book only touches the tip of the iceberg when it comes to things you can find while road-tripping US 395. If I were to write about all of the history, people, legends and lore of this beautiful area and highway, it would fill a tome to rival *War and Peace*. I hope you enjoyed this small piece of California legends, lore and tales of historic deeds.

BIBLIOGRAPHY

BOOKS

Clune, Brian with Bob Davis. *California's Historic Haunts*. Atglen, PA: Schiffer Books, 2014.

Nadler, Danielle. *Without a Trace: The Life of the Sierra Phantom*. Danielle Nadler, 2016.

Woodruff, David, and Gail Woodruff. *Tales along El Camino Sierra*. Gardnerville, NV: El Camino Sierra Publishing, 2017.

———. *Tales along El Camino Sierra Two*. Gardnerville, NV: El Camino Sierra Publishing, 2019.

———. *Tales along El Camino Sierra Three*. Gardnerville, NV: El Camino Sierra Publishing, 2020.

WEBSITES

Boron

Courtney, Carly. "Pancho Barnes: The Most Unladylike Aviatrix in History." Disciples of Flight. www.disciplesofflight.com.

Foulkes, Debbie. "Pancho Barnes (1901–1975)." Forgotten Newsmakers. March 16, 2011. https://forgottennewsmakers.com.

Mosley, Pat. "George Swain: 1919–2000." John Muir Association. www. johnmuir.org.

Roadside America. "Twenty Mule Team Museum." www.roadsideamerica.com.

Manzanar

Densho Encyclopedia. "Manzanar." www.encyclopedia.densho.org.

National Park Service. "Manzanar." www.nps.gov.

Burro Schmidt

Bickel Camp. "Burro Schmidt." www.bickelcamp.org.

McLellan, Dennis. "Evelyn 'Tonie' Seger, 95; Keeper of Tunnel in the Mojave Desert That Became a Tourist Draw." *Los Angeles Times*, June 15, 2003.

Schwartz, Scott. "Burro Schmidt's Tunnel." Desert USA. www.desertusa.com.

Bessie Brady

Millspaugh, Al. "The Saga of the Bessie Brady." Mt. Whitney Packers & Owens Valley History Site. www.owensvalleyhistory.com.

Mt. Whitney Packers & Owens Valley History Site. "Desert Steamer." www. owensvalleyhistory.com.

Lone Pine

California Curiosities. "Nightmare Rock." www.californiacuriosities.com.

Cerro Gordo Mines. http://cerrogordomines.com.

List Challenges. "Movies and TV Shows Shot in the Alabama Hills, Lone Pine, CA." www.listchallenges.com.

Lone Pine Chamber of Commerce. "History of the Lone Pine Area." https://lonepinechamber.org.

Museum of Western Film History. https://museumofwesternfilmhistory.org.

Nevada Appeal. "Finding Reminders of Owens Lake's Rich History." May 29, 2019. www.nevadaappeal.com.

Weird California. "Keeler." www.weirdca.com.
————. "Lone Pine: Movie Road." www.weirdca.com.
————. "Lone Pine Ghosts." www.weirdca.com.

Independence

Britannica. "Mary Austin." https://www.britannica.com.
Digital Desert. "Independence, California." www.digital-desert.com.
Fort Independence. "History." https://www.fortindependence.com.
Landmark Adventures. "Putnam's Cabin." June 16, 2011. http://landmarkadventures.blogspot.com.
Mountain Mouse Land. "Winnedumah Paiute Monument—Inyo Mountains." https://www.mtnmouse.com.
Ruhge, Justin. "Camp Independence." California State Military History and Museums Program. http://militarymuseum.org.
Sierra Nevada Geotourism. "Mary Austin's Home (No. 220 California Historical Landmark)." https://sierranevadageotourism.org.

Bodie Ghost Town

Bodie, California. "Bodie State Historic Park." https://www.bodie.com.
Bodie State Historic Park. https://www.parks.ca.gov.
Clune, Brian, and Bob Davis. *California's Historic Haunts*. Atglen, PA: Schiffer Books, 2014.

Tuttle Creek Ashram

The Franklin Merrell-Wolff Fellowship. "Tuttle Creek Ashram." http://www.merrell-wolff.org/ashrama.
Summit Post. "History of the Ashram." https://www.summitpost.org.

Ferris Wheel

Famous Inventors. "George Ferris." https://www.famousinventors.org.

Malanowski, Jamie. "The Brief History of the Ferris Wheel." *Smithsonian* (June 2015). https://www.smithsonianmag.com.

Norman Clyde

Alsup, William. "The Search for Peter Starr." Traditional Mountaineering. www.traditionalmountaineering.org.
Wheelock, Walt. "Norman Clyde." Mt. Whitney Packers & Owens Valley History Site. http://www.owensvalleyhistory.com.

Convict Lake

Convict Lake Resort. "About Us." https://convictlake.com.
Mammoth Lakes. "Convict Lake." http://www.mammothlakes.us.
Mammoth (CA) Times. "Book on Convict Lake Drowning Accident Both Heals, Hurts." February 2012. https://www.mammothtimes.com.

Mono Lake

Malloy, Betsy. "Reasons to Visit Odd and Interesting Mono Lake." TripSavvy. https://www.tripsavvy.com.
Mono County, California. "Mono Lake." https://www.monocounty.org.

Lost Cement Mine

Chalfant, Walter. "The Lost Cement Mines." Mt. Whitney Packers & Owens Valley History Site. www.owensvalleyhistory.com.
Excerpt taken from J.W.A. Wright. *Tales of the Pioneers*. Stanford, CA: Stanford University Press, 1942.
Legends of America. "Lost Cement Gold Mine of Mammoth Mountain, California." https://www.legendsofamerica.com.

Tom's Place

Tom's Place Resort. "The History of Tom's Place Resort." http://www.tomsplaceresort.com.

Lemoyne Hazard

California Peace Officers' Memorial Foundation. "Lemoyne A. Hazard." https://camemorial.org.
Mt. Whitney Packers & Owens Valley History Site. "Bishop Residents." http://owensvalleyhistory.com.

Nellie Bly Baker

Oklahoma Historical Society. "Baker O'Bryan, Nellie Bly (1895?–1984)." https://www.okhistory.org.

Bridgeport and the White Lady

Bridgeport Inn. "Area History." https://thebridgeportinn.com.
South Yuba River State Park. "Bridgeport History." https://www.southyubariverstatepark.org.

ABOUT THE AUTHOR

As the historian for Planet Paranormal and the Full Spectrum Project, Brian has traveled the entire state of California researching its haunted hot spots and historical locations in an effort to bring knowledge of the paranormal and the wonderful history of the state to those interested in learning.

His interest in history led him to volunteer aboard the USS *Iowa* and at the Fort MacArthur Military Museum. Brian travels the state giving lectures at colleges and universities and has been involved with numerous TV shows, including *Ghost Adventures*, *My Ghost Story*, *Dead Files* and *Ghost Hunters* and was the subject in a companion documentary for the movie *Paranormal Asylum*. He has also appeared on numerous local, national and international radio programs. Clune is the cohost for the radio program *The Full Spectrum Project*, which deals in subjects ranging from ghosts and true crime to all things odd and weird, both natural and supernatural.

His other books include *California's Historic Haunts* (Schiffer Books) and the highly acclaimed *Ghosts of the* Queen Mary (The History Press), as well as *Ghosts and Legends of Alcatraz* and *Ghosts and Legends of Calico*, all with coauthor Bob Davis. Brian and Bob also teamed up to write the riveting biography of "ghost box" creator Frank Sumption. Clune is also the author of *Haunted San Pedro* and *Hollywood Obscura*, the spellbinding book dealing with Hollywood's dark and sordid tales of murder and ghosts. He is currently working on the following books: *Murder and Mayhem in Hollywood*, *California's Haunted Route 66*, *Haunted Southern California*, *Haunted*

Northern California and a book about the cryptids of California, this with his son Carmel. His forthcoming book *Dark Tourism: California* will be released in the spring of 2022 by Schiffer Books.

Clune lives in Southern California with his loving wife, Terri, his three wonderful children and, of course, Wandering Wyatt!